SEA OF CORTEZ AND OTHER PLAYS

JOHN STEPPLING

Sea of Cortez

and Other Plays

*With an Appreciation
by Martin Epstein*

SUN & MOON PRESS
LOS ANGELES · 1996

Sun & Moon Press
A Program of The Contemporary Arts Educational Project, Inc.
a nonprofit corporation
6026 Wilshire Boulevard, Los Angeles, California 90036

This edition first published in paperback in 1996 by Sun & Moon Press
10 9 8 7 6 5 4 3 2 1
FIRST EDITION
© 1996 by John Steppling
Biographical material © 1996 by Sun & Moon Press

This book was made possible, in part, through an operational grant from
the Andrew W. Mellon Foundation, through a matching grant from
the National Endowment for the Arts, and through contributions to
The Contemporary Arts Educational Project, Inc., a nonprofit corporation.

Cover: Roy Lichtenstein, *Landscape 9,* 1967
Design: Katie Messborn
Typography: Guy Bennett

LIBRARY OF CONGRESS CATALOGING IN PUBLICATION DATA
Steppling, John [1951]
Sea of Cortez and Other Plays / John Steppling
p.cm—(Sun & Moon Classics 96)
ISBN: 1-55713-237-2
I. Title. II. Series.
PS3569.T3869S43 1996
812'.54—dc20
96-31616
CIP

Printed in the United States of America on acid-free paper.

In memory of my father,
Carl John Steppling

CONTENTS

John Steppling (*An Appreciation*)

Let the prospective reader be forewarned: there are two imminent dangers in dealing with the plays of John Steppling. Because of their seeming simplicity, you may be tempted to impose a fashionably minimalist interpretation on a landscape that is actually dazzling in its dramatic complexity. You also run the risk of falling from your own idea of how bad things can get into an imagined hell that makes you know you've arrived.

Steppling's plays have the same kind of visceral power found in the paintings of Francis Bacon. The actual beauty of their presence can only be experienced after one surrenders to the ways in which they lacerate. Driven by a verbal and visual intensity akin to Japanese Noh, Steppling's work presents a kind of American haunting, in which the characters, almost ghosts themselves, do everything they can to "hang in there" while an inexplicable black hole slowly sucks them into what, in more classical times, would be called "a destiny."

Here's Jack, the dog handler from *Standard of the Breed,* on the eve of having to turn his dogs loose in the Nevada desert: "I didn't want the dogs of the rich, of the aristocracy. I *chose* Mastiffs, they're common. I chose Mastiffs. [*pause*] Very powerful…."

Steppling's choice as a writer is synonymous with Jack's. He chooses the marginal, the dispossessed, characters so truly at the end of their rope, the effort they make merely to tell their stories seems to tax them beyond endurance. Impacting their silences together with their articulations, Steppling gives them a language that is as close to music as the spoken word can come. The more one rereads these plays (and one must reread them!), the more Steppling's abrasively lyrical dialogue acquires new meanings. Not to mention how painfully funny so many of his singular moments can be.

Meanwhile, Steppling has been writing and directing in the Los Angeles area for the last fifteen years, where he is recognized as a pre-eminent force in the L.A. theater scene. To date, he was written over thirty plays, and though his work has been produced in San Francisco, Louisville, New York, and London, Sun & Moon Press is to be congratulated for making his deeply moving and original voice available for further discovery.

MARTIN EPSTEIN
New York University

THE SHAPER

"...the sleeper, alone
Like a pilgrim on his pallet,
Unidentified corpse
—Dreams embodied by lucid Greek characters,
By the simple sacredness of two or three syllables,
As though full of the triumphant sun's whiteness—
Foretelling a reality
Matured in unseen depths and now ripe, like the sun
To be enjoyed or feared."

—PIER PAOLO PASOLINI
(McAfee trans.)

The Shaper was first presented at The Nighthouse in Los Angeles on November 2, 1984. The play was directed by John Steppling and had the following cast:

BUD	Lee Kissman
DEL	Scott Paulin
JILL	Laura Owens
SHERRY	Noreen Hennessy
REESA	Elizabeth Ruscio
FELIX	Jack Slater

ACT 1

SCENE 1

In the shop, late at night, after closing. BUD *is working at a table in rear.* JILL *and* SHERRY *are standing downstage.* SHERRY *is agitated, nervous, upset.*

Lights up.

SHERRY: What do I do next? You know Glenn Fischel? That's his lawyer, Del's lawyer. They're friends.

JILL: I don't know him.

SHERRY: I don't know, Christ.

JILL: I don't know the names of many lawyers.

Pause.

SHERRY: He's a friend of Del's. [*pause*] He's a big lawyer but him and Del are friends.

JILL: You got the number for him?

SHERRY: No, but I can call information. I can get it that way. I'll call in the morning. Del said if anything ever happened to him to call Glenn.

Pause.

You think they busted him with the coke on him?

JILL: I don't know, I guess.

SHERRY: I wonder what happened, you know?

JILL: Del wasn't stupid about that.

SHERRY: No. He thought of it as a business.

JILL: He always took care of business.

SHERRY: That's right, that's true.

13

JILL: I always felt that. I was impressed, always, how he kept it together, just a business, no fuckin' around.

SHERRY: I guess I can't think of anyone else. [*pause*] It's late now. I guess there's nothing more to do until tomorrow. [*pause*] I tried everyone I could think of. I tried everyone who I thought would have any money, who could lay their hands on any money. That's the problem isn't it, laying their hands on money. [*pause*] I guess there's no more to do tonight.

JILL: I don't think so. [*pause*] I don't think there is.

SHERRY: [*to* BUD] Thank god you and Del got this shop or I don't know what.

> *Pause.*

BUD: You own it. [*pause, thinking*] If you really own it.

SHERRY: Well you guys own it. That's playing it smart.

BUD: My Dad emphasized that. When he'd explain reality to us boys.

SHERRY: That's right.

BUD: Del and me were smart.

SHERRY: You did it right.

BUD: Yes we did.

> *Pause.* SHERRY *laughs small nervous laugh, then turns and walks downstage. She stands looking back over her shoulder at* BUD *and* JILL.

I wanted to make a point.

> *Long silence,* BUD *staring down,* JILL *watching him.*

I think she got part of it, don't you? I think I made a point.

> BUD *turns away and moves back to his work table. He starts to work then stops, listening, as though to a voice off somewhere to his left, stage right.*

JILL: What were you doing when you'd be in that old play house, old doll house for kids. In the backyard of our house on Freemont?

BUD: [*softly*] I know the one.

JILL: On your hands and knees, looking at the walls. This child's playhouse, deserted. Maybe four feet high, with a window, and a little doorway.

BUD: [*softly*] ...deserted?

Silence.

JILL: I hadn't seen you then for two years.

Silence.

BUD: That's six years ago.

Silence.

JILL: This isn't a nice world, I don't want to say so. But that's the way it is.

Lights out.

SCENE 2

In shop, REESA *is walking slowly between* JILL *and* SHERRY, *seated on chairs, and* BUD, *who is sitting on the edge of his work table.*

Lights up, quickly.

REESA: You've all got such great tans. All of you.

JILL: Not really—I mean it's winter right now.

REESA: Out here everyone has such incredible tanned skin, such rich color.

JILL: Not so much now, in winter.

REESA: These great copper and bronze shades to your skin, its so healthy looking, incredible.

REESA *stops walking, bends down next to* JILL.

REESA: Maybe, compared to where I come from, we're all

so pale—compared to that all of you out here look very athletic, or something. It makes men seem so vigorous.

REESA gets up and resumes pacing. She pauses and looks directly at BUD. JILL and SHERRY both see her. After a moment she turns and walks back downstage.

SHERRY: [*to REESA*] Del doesn't blame me does he?

Pause. REESA looks blankly at her.

[*to JILL*] I guess he's pissed at me now, not being able to get the money.

JILL: Del loves you.

SHERRY: I tried everyone. You know how many people I called. I tried everyone.

Silence.

[*to JILL but so everyone can hear her.*] I didn't know he had a sister. He never told me.

Long pause. REESA stares down at SHERRY, then turns and slowly walks upstage.

[*to JILL*] I didn't tell you, you know.

JILL: About what?

SHERRY: About his sister coming out.

JILL: Its OK.

SHERRY: I don't know why I didn't.

JILL: Its nothing. Nothing.

SHERRY: I felt so weird, I don't know how come. Are you mad?

JILL: Of course not.

SHERRY: I guess you'd have every right to be.

JILL: No.

SHERRY: He had to call his mother for the money. He had to call her from jail. I know he hates to have to ask her for anything.

Silence. SHERRY *turns toward* JILL, *leans in toward her.*

[*with venom*] What do you care—right?

JILL: [*surprised, hurt*] Sherry.

SHERRY: If you cared you would have done more.

JILL: Like what? [*pause, waiting*] Like fucking what?

> SHERRY *looks down, she's fighting back sobs. Lights fade out on* JILL *and* SHERRY. *Lights remain up on* BUD *and* REESA *at work table.*

REESA: I haven't seen Del since high school.

BUD: No?

REESA: No. Since I was in high school, he was already living out. [*pause*] I remember you.

BUD: Do you?

REESA: From Huntington, seventy-two.

BUD: Seventy-two. I was there.

REESA: I couldn't go much because of school.

BUD: Were you disappointed?

REESA: No, I wasn't, that wasn't it.

BUD: I didn't mean…

REESA: No, OK. OK, I mean I was only seventeen.

BUD: Del was at Huntington a lot.

REESA: Were you friends then?

BUD: Not then.

REESA: He said you were.

BUD: [*with an edge of anger—a little louder*] Well he's full of shit then. If that's what he said, he can't remember shit, that's all. No way Del was a friend of mine, no way, not in 1972.

> *Lights fade out.*

SCENE 3

Shop, day, rack of surf boards on the stage left wall. FELIX *is looking them over.* BUD *comes over. Lights up.*

BUD: Looking for a new stick?

FELIX: Oh, no, no, not really. [*extends hand*] I'm Felix Carbahaul, Sherry's ex-husband.

BUD: [*shakes*] Right, how are you.

FELIX: Fine, fine thank you.

BUD: What's your name?

FELIX: Felix, Felix Carbahaul.

BUD: Oh right, yeah.

FELIX: You know, some guys I know said to check out this place if I was thinkin' of getting somethin'.

BUD: Fine, fine, OK Felix, you see the thing of it is—my name's on every board here.

FELIX: Uh huh.

BUD: People see this name...[*points to name on board*] they know its a reliable stick.

FELIX: That's what these guys I know said.

BUD: Bud Westly...right there, see? [*points to name on board*] There it is.

FELIX: Hmmm-hmmm.

BUD: My name—Bud Westly. [*short pause*] You see?

BUD *points at another board—where his name is.*

FELIX: Right off I kinda figured that's who you were.

BUD *puts arm around* FELIX'S *shoulder.*

BUD: The terrible part though, Felix, the truly terrible part is that I see this place catch fire every night— whoosh—it goes up like a thatched hut. Or...or like a match stick house, house made of match sticks.

[*pause*] ...Like a hillside of dry grass. [*snaps fingers*] Just like that, once it catches, it goes like that. [*snaps fingers again*]

    Pause. BUD *stares at* FELIX.

I'm half owner. I'm half owner of this place. [*pause*] Del made me a partner—it was my name. [*pause*] Felix?

FELIX: What?

BUD: You know Jill right?

FELIX: Jill? No, uh huh.

BUD: [*pause*] She won't wait it out, she won't, I can see that, I can see that she can't let go. [*pause*] Jill is my wife—I don't mean married or any of that shit—but she's my wife, my *wife*. [*pause*] That's the other terrible part Felix, there's two terrible parts, this is the other part, the other terrible part.

    BUD *pulls away. Silence.*
    Lights out.

SCENE 4

    Early evening, rear of shop. BUD *in mask, gloves, etc., working on board.* FELIX *stands off to the side, watching, a drink in hand. He's half drunk and getting more so.*

    Lights up.

FELIX: I came as a favor...you following me?

    Pause.

Nothing said I had to do this...All right then?!

    Pause, takes a long gulp of drink—shudders.

Ughh...[*pause*] Do you think it's crazy for ex-husbands, or, or ex-wives, whatever. Whatever. You think it's, you know, to come around your ex's.

Pause. BUD *keeps working.*

Some might say I'm pussy whipped.

Waits for a response. BUD *keeps working a moment, then stops, takes off mask, looks over at* FELIX. *Pause.*

Do you think that?

BUD: No, I don't think you're pussy whipped.

Pause. BUD *pulls back on mask and starts working again.*

FELIX: I'm a pretty fair judge of the opposite sex. [*pause*] And, Bud? [*short pause*] They don't deserve to be treated on the square.

FELIX *gulps down remainder of drink.*
Lights fade...

SCENE 5

Shop, night. REESA *is wearing a walkman.*
Lights up.

REESA: I want you to hear something.

She takes off walkman and starts to hand it to BUD.

BUD: What?

REESA: I want you to hear this song.

BUD *won't take walkman.*

[*pause*] You don't like Rock 'n Roll. I know that. OK.
Pause.

BUD: I don't want to hear anything right now.

REESA: I like my certain tapes, you know, every morning I listen, on my earphones, I need it to wake me up.

Pause. She looks at him.

It's Peter Gabriel.

BUD: Who's Peter Gabriel?

REESA: I need it to wake up. Music helps me wake up.
I don't care what you think.

BUD: I don't think anything.

REESA: This girl I used to model with, she wore a
walkman in the dressing room all the time—I know
it's obnoxious, but I can't help that.

BUD: Peter Gabriel isn't rock?

REESA: I only listen to like, five tapes, the Isley Brothers, Weather Report, Peter Gabriel, Julio Iglesias, and
Teddy Pendergrass. And sometimes George Benson,
and sometimes Flock of Seagulls. [*pause*] I watch MTV
too, so fuck it, you know?!

BUD: OK, but Reesa…

REESA: [*cuts him off*] My older sister's friends, and Del,
I've got this reputation in my family for being a gos-
sip, and also for having no sense of humor.

BUD: I never heard that.

REESA: [*edge of hostility*] You've got your little Jill and
your other little chickies, well I'm not some sixteen-
year-old fuck you know.

BUD: What are you talking about?

REESA: Right. I'm nine years older than sixteen.

> REESA *grabs both of his arms at the wrists and
> starts to suck on his neck.* BUD *pulls free.*

What'll Jill and your little twisters say about a love
bite—I don't call them hickies, I like what the English
call them, love bites, I'll give you a whopper love
bite…

> *She lunges at him, trying to suck on his neck.*
> BUD *resists, shoves her away, but she keeps trying.*

BUD *gradually relaxes and slowly falls to the floor,*
REESA *astride him, sucking feverishly on his neck.*
Lights fade out.

SCENE 6
Shop, night. BUD *finishing up work on boards.*
JILL *enters.*
Lights up.

JILL: You were up all night. [*pause*] You worked all night.
Long pause.

How's your back?

BUD: What do you mean?

JILL: Your back.

BUD: My back what?

Pause. They look at each other.

[*cuts her off*] My back is fine—strong as ever—nothing the matter with it, nothing.

Pause.

Foam dust...[*waves hand over dust on board*]
...breathing foam dust, well, there's something—it's
highly injurious to inhale this shit. I'm always very
careful about wearing my mask...

JILL: [*cuts him off, louder*] You worked all night—you
worked all fucking night! [*pause, calms down a little*]
You never got to sleep—asshole.

BUD *throws his mask, hard, from very close range,*
at JILL. *She ducks but it hits her.*

Long, frozen silence, eyes on each other.

You're trying to sell Felix a board—that's great man,
real class Bud—he has a game leg, asshole—you
asshole. You asshole. Big fucking asshole. He can't
even walk ri...

BUD *takes apron from the table where he placed it after removing it at top of scene, and hits* JILL, *hard and repeatedly as she crouches and attempts to cover up.* BUD *stops suddenly, staring down at* JILL *on floor. She is breathing hard, on hands and knees. He slowly, calmly puts apron on top of work table, then picks up mask and places it next to apron.* JILL *remains on hands and knees trying to catch her breath. She doesn't look at* BUD. *He walks slowly downstage. Light on* JILL *fades out, though she doesn't move. Light comes up downstage as* BUD *walks into it.* SHERRY *is seated in a wooden chair, stage left. She is holding a can of beer—which she sips from. She speaks facing audience, not looking at* BUD, *who is behind and to her left.*

SHERRY: I saw my father today. He hadn't changed his bandages once, not once. [*pause*] They were dirty. They're for his fingers. It's hard when I don't see him every day, but I just can't. [*pause*] That would be impossible.

    BUD *steps closer, stops. Pause.*

I let her out.

BUD: How'd you know? [*pause*] I mean...

SHERRY: [*cuts him off*] I went over and let her out.

BUD: Thanks.

SHERRY: Hey?!...Hey!...Hey, she understands. [*short pause*] Bud? Hey, you know that? 'Cause she does—all the way—she understands.

BUD: We used to live together.

SHERRY: I know. I used to come over to your house. On Freemont.

BUD: Yes.

SHERRY: I know it.

BUD: It never worked—it was a fucking hassle—which I don't need. One thing I don't need.

BUD moves closer, looks down at SHERRY.

We fucked once—you remember?

SHERRY: In high school. That's like different people.

BUD: Same people.

Long pause.

SHERRY: I can't remember how it was.

BUD: I got on top of you but you didn't like it—so we switched—I fucked you from behind. In your apartment.

Pause.

SHERRY: I don't like talking about that.

BUD: OK. OK. [*pause*] But that's how it was.

SHERRY: Why do you want to talk like this?

BUD steps away. Pause.

BUD: Age has a lot to do with it. [*He pulls on several hairs on front of his head.*] Even at thirty-six… [*looks at his torso—lifts shirt, looks at stomach*] …I see change.

Pause. He looks at SHERRY.

I had a chance to get into modeling once. This guy I met playing volleyball—this is ten years ago—twelve years ago. Why am I bringing it up?

BUD waits for answer. Pause.

You let her out? Why did you come right at that time?

SHERRY: I just did. I came over and I unlocked the closet and I let her out.

BUD: Was she in there for very long?

SHERRY: No.

BUD: You think you could die locked in a closet?

SHERRY: No, not that one. It's got a little window. That's
how I heard her—through the window to outside—to
the driveway. No, you couldn't die—unless it was for
weeks and you starved.

Lights out.

SCENE 7

Shop, night, dim light. BUD *asleep in chair.* REESA
enters, quietly—creeping up on him. JILL *enters from
other room, stage left of shop.* REESA *and* JILL *see
each other. They hold for a moment, then* REESA
continues over to BUD. *He remains asleep as* REESA
runs her hand lightly around his neck and hair.
JILL *steps closer, eyes on* REESA.

Lights up.

REESA: Del gets released tonight...this morning, they
said it takes five hours sometimes—five hours.

JILL: It's morning now isn't it?

REESA: Is it? Can you believe they take five hours just
to let you go?

JILL: What's another couple hours—you know?!

REESA *steps away from the still sleeping* BUD.

REESA: I got a cassette of me and this guy Joel on Dance
Fever, that TV show, we were contestants—dance contestants, you seen that show?

JILL: You were gonna show Bud?

REESA: I told him about it—we didn't win but you know
that was because this faggot they had as a judge
didn't like this guy I was with—Joel—you know, he
wasn't a judge every week, not regular on the show—
I guess he was a guest judge—and they have like three

    categories they judge you for…Except it's all bullshit
    'cause they wouldn't show Joel the judge cards after-
    wards.

JILL: This judge didn't like Joel?

REESA: I think so, maybe he was trying to flirt with him.

JILL: The judge?

REESA: The judge—yeah—was flirting sort of with Joel—
    and Joel gave him this mean look. I told him that was
    gonna blow it for us too.

        Pause.

    What is ironic—you know—what is ironic is that Joel
    is a kind of faggot now anyway.

        Pause. JILL *steps closer to* REESA.

JILL: You really are Del's sister.

REESA: What in the heck does that mean? [*pause*] You
    think, what?

JILL: Just a thought—maybe you weren't really his sis-
    ter.

REESA: Oh.

JILL: No offense.

REESA: Huh? No.

JILL: I've got to go.

        Pause.

    Is Del coming here?

REESA: I suppose he is.

        JILL *suddenly gives* REESA *a big hug, squeezing
    hard, then lets go.*

JILL: [*pause*] That's for Del.

        Pause. They look at each other. JILL *turns and
    exits.* REESA *runs after her, grabs her arm just at
    exit to street.*

REESA: [*pause*] Does Bud have a video cassette player?
   ...I forgot to ask him.
JILL: I don't think so.
REESA: Oh. [*pause*] That's a shame.
      Pause.
JILL: Why don't you suck his cock... He'll like that.
      She exits.
REESA: [*pause*] Bye Jill.
      Lights out.

   SCENE 8
   Outside county jail, front edge of stage. SHERRY
   and FELIX *standing in coats buttoned up against
   the chill.*
   Lights up.
FELIX: I didn't have to come—just because you called—
   that doesn't mean I had to come.
SHERRY: I know.
      Pause.
FELIX: I was glad to be able to help—don't get me
   wrong—I was glad to do it.
      Silence.
   I missed two days work coming all the way out here.
SHERRY: I'm sorry you had to do that.
FELIX: No—no, it was my choice all the way—see I'm
   not like that.
SHERRY: [*pause*] ...like what?
FELIX: [*turns away, takes a step*] When the fuck do they
   release him? This is crazy—we been waiting for a half-
   hour.
SHERRY: They said it could take hours.

Pause. FELIX *turns away disgusted. Walks back and forth along length of playing area.*

FELIX: What did I say when you called? Huh?

SHERRY: I don't remember exactly Felix.

FELIX: I offered the money—you didn't even have to ask.

SHERRY: I know.

FELIX: Oh, I mean I know, I know, it wasn't that much— I know it wasn't enough...

SHERRY: ...Please Felix.

FELIX: Did you tell your friends that?

SHERRY: Tell them what?

FELIX: [*turns away*] At least I never got put in jail.

SHERRY: What's wrong with you?

FELIX: [*pause, looking at her*] Don't...don't, ah—just...go off on something...OK?! [*pause*] Sherry...OK?

FELIX *turns away again and nervously paces up and back length of stage.* SHERRY *sits, wearily, on wooden bench, far edge, stage right. Long silence.*

SHERRY: It can take hours sometimes.

FELIX: [*stops*] What?

SHERRY: The cop at the desk in there said it can take hours sometimes—if it's crowded.

FELIX: To let him out?

SHERRY: Yeah, but it doesn't seem very crowded now.

Pause. FELIX *stands looking down at floor. He looks over at* SHERRY.

FELIX: Del can't keep this up, we both know that, right?

SHERRY: [*tired of talking*] Oh god—who knows—ask him, ask Del.

FELIX: I could talk to him... or, I don't know, it's a stu-

pid idea maybe? [*pause*] I could tell him about cable
TV—it's wide open right now, but you can bet that's
not goin' to last—now's the time—the chance is there
if you go after it. I can answer his questions, up to a
point—then you go sit down with a district sales su-
pervisor.

> *Pause.*

Of course, maybe he's not into that kind of thing,
some people aren't—aren't comfortable with "sales"
[*pause*] I could be making a fool of myself—Sherry?
Couldn't I?... Sherry?

> *He looks at* SHERRY *who stares blankly back at*
> *him.*
>
> *Lights out.*

SCENE 9

> *Shop, night.* REESA *sits on floor with walkman*
> *on.* JILL *is offstage left, kitchen.* BUD *stands behind*
> *and to left, stage left, of* REESA. *He is combing his*
> *hair.* REESA *turns around and looks at him. She*
> *takes off earphones.*

REESA: In Ohio—um, where I lived, Del would write us
letters—to my family—and me—he'd write us from
here. [*pause*] The Ohio Valley, um...is just the stink
hole of all time—of everywhere—the worst. [*pause*]
Del's letters always mentioned you—and my mother
would want to know about who you were...she,
ah...would ask me.

> JILL *enters with a box of donuts and paper cups*
> *of coffee. She sets box on floor next to* REESA *and*
> *sits down.*

That was friendly...[*grabs donut and takes a bite*] bringing donuts, what a friendly thing to do.

JILL: I bought a variety.

REESA: No twists?

> JILL *stares at her without answering. Pause.*

[*to* BUD] You sure picked a friendly girl... Bud, you picked a very, very friendly girl for a girlfriend–[*to* JILL] I like twists best of any donuts–but isn't that the way, if that's what you like then that's gonna be the one that gets forgot.

JILL: I bought a variety.

REESA: I was just telling Bud–before you came with the donuts–I was saying how my mother would ask me, um, after we'd read all Del's letters...ah, she'd ask me to tell her about Bud.

> *Pause.* JILL *continues to sip coffee and eat a donut ignoring* REESA. BUD *remains on table–no eating or drinking.*

My family, see, live in Ohio–in the Ohio Valley–well, I should explain, God, I mean these letters, the way it made Bud seem–how–um, he sounded like a movie star almost... [*turns to Bud*] Don't you want a jelly donut? We got chocolate and jelly left–and a buttermilk. [*pause*] Bud?

BUD: No apple fritters?

REESA: I don't see any, no.

> *Pause.*

[to JILL] I guess my mother–who still lives in this cess pool town–in this dirtball house–to her, to Mom, you can see, you can see that Bud would seem like a movie star?

JILL: Well what did you tell your mother?

REESA: What did I tell her? This woman, this woman who, who has, now, a nearly bald head—this woman, this pig of a woman who dribbles when she eats and who moans all night with her angina—what could I tell such a person? ...A person asking me to talk about Bud...can you imagine a more obscene situation?

JILL: I can't imagine.

REESA: What did I tell her? Well, well, I...ah explained, you know, I explained that Bud was like a golden boy—like this shiny golden beach boy, that's what I said, I think—isn't that funny?

JILL: No.

REESA: Oh, well, Jill, this is Ohio—really disgusting filthy Ohio—don't you see? Ohio. [*pause*] This was Ohio. How could I explain California beaches to this crude dribbling pig-woman?

JILL: You'll say anything.

REESA: I won't.

JILL: You'll say anything.

REESA: I won't say anything. [*pause*] I won't say anything.

JILL *and* REESA *stare at each other. Silence.*

I remember *you*—I do.

JILL: You can't remember *me*.

REESA: A whole group of us girls—from high school, you know?! We hated you.

JILL: Don't say things that aren't true.

REESA: I remember seeing you—sitting on a beach towel—watching Bud out in the water. You were smoking a cigarette—and you knew that Bud would come right to you as soon as he came out of the water.

JILL: You're confused.

REESA: No. No...um...all of us girls, we would make up names for you, we would always call you by these awful names when we spoke about you.

JILL: After so many years I think it would be easy to get confused—I think you're confusing me with some-one else—with some other girl.

REESA: No...No, I remember—really, really.

Silence.

JILL *looks away from* REESA *over to* BUD.

JILL: [*to* BUD] Honey?

Silence.

Honey...? Your coffee...Don't want your coffee?

BUD *says nothing—sits silently.*

Lights fade out.

ACT 2

> *Shop, late night.* DEL *sits on wooden chair, facing audience. Behind him at table* BUD *stands, wearing apron, mask, shirt, etc., holding shaping tool in hand, but looking down at* DEL.

DEL: Those percodan, the girl photographer sold them, four dollars each, Christ, Christ—and gettin' wound up every night…it was pretty clean coke, it was. I felt like an old man, I'd trade anything I had, or got, for a successful bowel movement. Man has three stages, first stage young man will do anything for sex, second, the man does anything to make money, and third the old man will do anything for a good shit. [*longer pause, smiles at story*] Believe it or not I tried using a corkscrew to pull out this turd—the doctor in jail said I had "impacted feces," how's that?! But now it's almost the other extreme… Bud?! …I 'bout live on it—two, three bottles a week, I keep the Kaopectate people in business. [*pause*] I can't, not all the time… I'm not in control of my bladder. Less,…less frequent. Less frequent…[*short pause*]…less frequent.

> *Silence. Then* BUD *turns and starts to work, planing board.* DEL *stands and slowly walks back to table—he stands behind* BUD, *stage left of him.* BUD *continues to work, concentrating on the board.* DEL *watches; wraps his arms around himself, then hugs*

> *himself, rocking slightly on his feet. He hugs himself*
> *several times, gently–tenderly almost, very quietly.*
> *Lights fade out.*

SCENE 2
> *Shop, night.*
> *Lights up.*

DEL: It's the right way.

BUD: I understand.

DEL: I wanted to, face to face, in person.

BUD: Whatever you say, that's good enough.

DEL: Still, you can see where I'm comin' from, still, OK, still I wanted to let you know, in person. [*pause*] Tell you my feelings about all that's happened.

> *Pause.*

How do you feel? Are you not feeling good?

BUD: No, it's fine.

> DEL *puts his arm around* BUD's *shoulder.*

DEL: Don't lie to me on this–but you're feeling good then, that's what you're saying?

BUD: I'm feeling good, yeah.

> *Long pause.* DEL *paces a few steps back and forth.*

Nobody knows who I am anymore.

> DEL *stops, looks at floor, pause.*

DEL: It isn't helping–for right now, talking over those kind of things...not here, not now, for you, for your...sake, your...peace of mind.

BUD: I can't help it. [*pause*] Not all the time.

> *Pause.*

DEL: I'm just not going to go to jail. [*pause*] I won't–not a day. I won't go, that's all there is to that.

Pause.

I wanted to tell you—face to face, just us.

BUD: I know it.

DEL: Right in person, that's the way.

BUD: That's the way.

Pause.

DEL: It's going to cost me—but it pays off in the end—a quality attorney. [*pause*] But good ones cost. [*pause*] You get what you pay for with lawyers.

Lights out.

SCENE 3

Shop, very dim, day. BUD *and* DEL *seated, one on table, one on chair. Long silence as they sit quietly. Knock at door, offstage. Pause. Both freeze, listening. Another knock, then another, several more, then silence. After a moment both relax.*

DEL: [*quietly*] You awake?

BUD: Yeah.

Pause. JILL *enters from rear.* BUD *and* DEL *seem to come alive at sight of* JILL.

JILL: Why didn't you answer when I knocked?

BUD *looks away.* DEL *stands, ignores question by brushing off his pants.*

Why are you closed? You haven't opened all week. And the windows are all covered with tin foil.

JILL *looks from one to the other, waiting for an answer. Silence.*

DEL: Is it still morning?

JILL *looks at him but says nothing.*

Jill, what's the time?

JILL: [*looks at watch*] Two-fifteen.

> DEL *nods, then turns away and walks around table to rear. He rubs his face and eyes with hands.*

It's like an oven in here.

> BUD *nods vaguely.* JILL *looks back at* DEL, *then back over at* BUD. *Silence. She pulls up a chair and sits.*

On the way here, just now, driving over—I ran over a cat. [*pause*] God it was awful—you could hear the crunch, I swear. When I looked in the rear view mirror I saw it kicking, furiously, kicking its rear leg. I drove on quickly. I thought I should go back and put it out of its pain. I drove off instead. I was afraid to go back and have to look at it.

DEL: It was probably already dead.

JILL: But it was kicking. Jerky kinds of kicking.

DEL: That can happen—in fact it's common.

JILL: The kicking? After they're dead?

DEL: I'd say it happens more often than not.

JILL: Kicking? After they're dead?

DEL: I think so, yeah.

JILL: I feel like a murderer. [*pause*] Is that silly?

> *Lights out.*

SCENE 4

> *Lights up. Shop, evening.* DEL *standing with fifth of vodka in one hand, glass of orange juice in the other. He pours generous shot of vodka into glass. Off stage left we hear voices, somewhat muffled, indistinct, of* SHERRY, JILL, REESA. FELIX *enters from left.* DEL *hands him the vodka and OJ.*

DEL: You know why they're called screwdrivers?

  FELIX *takes sip, waits for answer.*

Steel workers drank vodka, they used to anyway, and they started puttin' it in containers of OJ—on the job—and they would actually stir 'em with their screwdrivers. That's a fact.

  FELIX *sits.* SHERRY *enters from left.*

FELIX: [*to* DEL, *primarily*] Today, shit, me and Sherry, we were eating lunch—the two of us, and this seagull...[*to* Sherry] right?...this seagull...

  FELIX *starts acting out his story.*

...He's just cruising along, and he circles over us a couple times and then he just sails along the top of this chain link fence—like fifteen feet high maybe—just gliding along, and right when he's above us he drops his load—a perfect fuckin' shot, and lucky for us the wind—we had enough of a wind, it blew it over the fence, otherwise we're goners. [*brief laugh*]

DEL: [*big smile*] Close call?!

FELIX: A perfect shot, like he was aiming. [*short laugh*]

DEL: Like he was, yeah.

FELIX: Maybe he practices. [*chuckles*]

  DEL *goes to table in rear and gets glass of o.j. He brings it to* SHERRY...

DEL: Well,...sounds like you dodged the bullet, eh? [*smiles*]

  SHERRY *sullenly accepts drink.*

FELIX: Del...I, ah...[*short pause*] I was think'n—I'd be interested, if you're still in "operation"—[*smile*]—I would be interested in picking up a bit of that "marching powder."

DEL: We'll talk later, no problem—we'll talk it over, anything you want—somewhere quiet—so we can have some privacy—how's that sound?

FELIX: Great—great. I hear what you're sayin', really man, I'm not into mickey mouse shit.

> *Abruptly* SHERRY *stands.* FELIX *and* DEL *stop and look at her. Pause.* SHERRY *then takes huge gulp of her drink, coughing afterwards. She then quickly begins to gulp more.* DEL *steps over next to her and pats her on the back as she breaks into severe fit of coughing and gagging.* FELIX *stands to get out of way of* SHERRY *who is also spilling much of her drink.*

DEL: [*tenderly, sweetly, exaggerated*] Take it easy…[*slapping her on back*]…come on…there…you got to watch that…huh? …Sweetheart? …Taking it a little too fast there weren't you?!

> SHERRY *gradually recovers.* DEL *puts his arm lightly around her shoulders.*

OK now? [*short pause*] Drink some water…in the kitchenette there's some Sparklett's, a jug of Sparklett's drinking water—very good, very fresh tasting…

> DEL *gently pushing* SHERRY *toward left exit.*

Okay?…that's the girl…go on baby…

SHERRY *jerks away from* DEL—*turns and looks at him, then at* FELIX, *then back at* DEL.

Del…oh…

> DEL *starts to usher her out once again…*

DEL: That's it…go on…go on…

> SHERRY *puts up mild resistence…but exits, left.*
> FELIX *sits back down, takes a long swallow of his*

drink. BUD *enters from outside, he's carrying a can of resin which he puts down on table.* DEL *goes over to table and hands* BUD *a "screwdriver."*

[*indicates can of resin*] What's that?

BUD: I ran out of resin.

DEL: Shit.

BUD: What?

DEL: I don't know.

BUD: I ran out, so I bought some more.

DEL: You going to start work on some boards.

> *Pause.*

Huh? What—we got some orders you haven't showed me?

> BUD *turns away and walks over next to* FELIX, *sits down.* SHERRY *enters with* JILL. *Nobody says anything.*

Hey, let's go to the porno movies.

> DEL *walks over to* JILL *and* SHERRY.

Starts at ten-thirty. Come on.

SHERRY: You know I don't want to go. I told you..

DEL: You told me—yeah what? You ever seen these movies?

SHERRY: I don't like that stuff.

DEL: Why you making a big deal out of this?

> DEL *waits for a moment for an answer, then turns away. He looks over at* FELIX...

You want to go?

FELIX: [*uncomfortable, glances at* SHERRY] ...Ah...sure ...sure.

> FELIX *stands, wobbly.*

DEL: All right! [*to* JILL]—what about you?...Jill?

JILL *looks over at* BUD, *then at* SHERRY...

JILL: You want to go, maybe,...Sherry?

SHERRY *says nothing. Silence.* JILL *and* BUD *exchange glances,* FELIX *and* SHERRY. DEL *goes over to* BUD.

DEL: You're comin' right?

BUD: I don't know.

DEL *turns away in disgust.*

DEL: [*under his breath*] For Christ's sake...

DEL *goes and gets his jacket.*

[*to* JILL] Come on—let's go.

JILL: I'm going to stay with Sherry, I think.

FELIX *puts on his coat.*

FELIX: Which films are these?

DEL: I don't know—"Trick Time" or something—I forget the other one.

FELIX *pauses.* DEL *goes over to* BUD.

[*intimate*] Hey Bud...Let's get out of here...you and me...Huh? Just you and me.

They look at each other for a long time.

Come on...Go get hammered.

BUD *gets up, puts on jacket—he starts out.*
SHERRY *steps over to* DEL.

SHERRY: As soon as I say something—I wish I hadn't—it sounds stupid. I think in my head—what I want to say and it sounds OK—not something smart but how I feel—then when I say it I know it sounds stupid.

DEL: I...I don't know Sherry...ah...Are you asking me something?

SHERRY: You guys—please Del—

DEL: Did I invite you over here? Did I?

SHERRY *says nothing. Silence.*

FELIX: "Trick Time."

DEL: Yeah?

FELIX: Well, isn't that a faggot movie?

DEL: Huh? No, no, uh uh.

FELIX: You sure?

DEL: No man—it's no faggot movie.

> *Pause.*

[*to* FELIX] Hey why don't you stay with the girls—I'd appreciate it.

> DEL *and* BUD *hurriedly exit.* FELIX *slowly slumps into chair. Long silence.*

FELIX: That's a faggot movie.

JILL: You're confused.

> *Silence.*

FELIX: You know the expression...Jill, the expression: "stirring the fudge"?

> JILL *stares at him.*
> *Lights out.*

SCENE 5

> *Lights up. Alley, front edge of playing area, night.* DEL *and* BUD, *both a little out of breath,* BUD *more so as he enters. Both dressed in jackets and knit caps.*

DEL: What happened?

BUD: Nothing. What do you mean?

DEL: What'd she do? [*short pause*] Jesus.

> DEL *walks a few steps, comes back.*

What was it? She wouldn't do what you said?

BUD: I got it. Christ.

DEL: You got it?! You did it—it was OK? She did it all?
> BUD *walks across stage to extreme left.* DEL *follows, stopping a moment to look behind—in direction* BUD *entered from.*

So, what is it?

BUD: [*irritated*] What?

DEL: [*angrier*] Well something fuckin' came down. It took forever, so what the fuck was it?

BUD: Shit. [*pause*] Aw shit, God Del...Damnit, damnit, damnit. Damnit!
> BUD *looks at* DEL, *pause.*

DEL: So?
> *Pause.*

Fuck. [*pause*] Forever. It felt like forever out here.
> *Pause.*

What'd she say?

BUD: She said OK. I told her to open the safe. She said OK and then we opened it.
> BUD *takes out money bags. Pause.*

DEL: Count it.

BUD: I don't want to count it.

DEL: You wanna know what we got?

BUD: Yeah.
> *Pause.*

DEL: You want me to count it?

BUD: I don't care.

DEL: I'll count it, OK? [*pause*] All right?
> BUD *walks a few feet off.* DEL *begins counting the bills.*
> *Lights fade out.*

SCENE 6
Lights up. Shop, night.

DEL: You were very cool. This slow walk, casual, not the kind of guy who hurries—[*pause*] I didn't think you'd done it.

BUD: I didn't point it—I gave her a glimpse in my bag, opened the flap, let her look in.

DEL: She knew when she peeped it. [*short pause*] Bet your ass—got her attention in a hurry—army issue .45 automatic.

    Pause.

You load the gun?

BUD: Did I load it?

DEL: Yeah—was the gun loaded?

BUD: What do you mean?

DEL: When you went in—did you have a loaded gun? Did it have bullets in it?

BUD: [*short pause*] No I didn't put in any bullets.

DEL: [*pause*] I don't get that. [*pause*] Like trying to fuck with a limp dick.

    Long pause.

BUD: You're right. Going in that way.

DEL: You got to do something like this all the way.

BUD: I know that. I didn't think I'd use them.

DEL: It's protection—it's insurance, for you. For both of us.

BUD: I pray we never use them. I pray to Christ.

DEL: [*Pause*] In a situation—the unexpected—I'm not laying some heavy thing on you here.

    DEL *sits down next to* BUD, *their shoulders touching. Silence.*

You don't want this anymore—say so and it's over—no bad feelings. We end the partnership right here and now.

> *Silence.* DEL *leans over, shoulder against* BUD. *Their faces almost touching.*

[*quiet*] That's one thing—all right, I can see what space you can get yourself into—but inside information is a whole other ride at the fair.

BUD: This is Reesa?

DEL: That's right.

> *Pause.*

I jumped at it, when she told me—shit, it's a gift, I mean it's fuckin' gift wrapped.

BUD: You want me to ask you about this?!

DEL: I would like you to think about it.

BUD: She's only been there a week.

DEL: She saw an opportunity—she fell into something—she saw there was an opportunity, that's all. [*pause*] Dumb luck, call it what you like.

> *Long silence.* DEL *reaches over and picks something out of* BUD'S *ear.*

You got all this foam shit in your ear.

> DEL *gently holds* BUD'S *shoulder with one hand while he picks out fiberglass shavings from his ear with the other.*

There...let's see the other one.

> BUD *turns head—*DEL *examines other ear.*

Winter swell's coming in—blowin' out today but was a good six feet, six and a half.

> DEL *finishes.*

BUD: I went down this morning and watched. [*pause*]

There were eight foot sets early, six thirty. A couple
guys were out but it was all junk—choppy—
>*Pause.*

DEL: [*quietly*] We have no idea what we're doing. [*pause*]
We've no idea of what could come down behind this—
[*vague smile, silent laugh*]
>*Pause.* BUD *looks at* DEL *who has head down.*
>*He starts massaging* DEL'S *neck, slowly.*

But I don't feel it—I can't seem to get a good hold on
it all…I mean…I know, I know about being in over
your head.
>BUD *pushes hair off* DEL'S *forehead and then runs*
>*his hand through his hair once.* BUD *then stops,*
>*stands up, looking around.*

What?

BUD: [*softly*] I think we're on fire—[*short pause*] The shop
has caught on fire.
>DEL *looks around, concerned, then confused.*

DEL: Hey Bud, what is this?
>BUD *sits back down.*

BUD: Let it go—it's nothing, nothing.
>*Lights fade out.*

SCENE 7
>*Lights up, shop, night.* DEL *and* BUD, *both stand-*
>*ing near table.* DEL *with drink in hand. Silence for*
>*a moment. Then sound of glasses and dishes rat-*
>*tling off stage. Both men react to sound, then look at*
>*each other.* BUD *speaks in hushed tone, not wanting*
>*whoever is out of room to hear.*

BUD: It makes me sick.

DEL: Stop it. [*pause*] It's in your head. That's where.

BUD: I'll be forty—

DEL: Not for four years.

BUD: It doesn't feel good—I can tell you.

> *Pause. More noise off stage.*

You kept in shape.

> DEL *looks at him,* BUD *looks away. Silence.*

DEL: I didn't set this up—[*nods toward offstage noise*]—if that's what you think.

BUD: Who cares what I think.

DEL: Is that what you think?

BUD: I look old, *old*!

DEL: [*pause*] You want me to talk to her?

> *Pause.* BUD *doesn't answer.*

What is this? You think I'm setting you up for something? [*pause*] It was her idea.

> REESA *enters with bowl of popcorn.* DEL *takes a handful—*BUD *refuses.* REESA *sits down with bowl in front of her.* BUD *turns and moves a few feet off.*

REESA: I am an expert with popcorn.

DEL: Tastes like it—tastes like it. [*turns to* BUD] You should taste some of this popcorn—first rate, Bud, first rate.

> BUD *turns and faces them.*

BUD: I'm not hungry.

REESA: Just a bite—I really wanted you to taste some. I made it for you—you've got to try some.

> *Pause,* DEL *and* REESA *staring at* BUD. *Sound of phone ringing offstage.* BUD *turns and looks offstage in direction of ringing.* DEL *looks offstage, then back at* BUD. REESA *keeps eyes on* BUD. *After two more rings* BUD *starts to take a step...*

DEL: [*louder*] This popcorn...[*back to normal*] it's excellent—you can't pass it up.

> BUD *stops, looking at* DEL. *Phone continues to ring.*

REESA: Let it ring.

BUD: It's the phone.

DEL: You have to try some.

> DEL *grabs handful of popcorn and offers it in outstretched hand to* BUD.

REESA: [*to* BUD] I know it's the phone.

DEL: [*to* BUD] Take a mouthful. [*Simultaneous*]

REESA: I can tell what a phone sounds like.

DEL: You'll hurt her feelings. [*Simultaneous*]

> *Phone rings once more*—BUD *has impulse to move to go answer it, but checks himself—eyes riveted on* DEL—*who is now smiling—large, artificial smile. Phone stops ringing. Silence.* REESA *gets up.*

REESA: Anyone want a soda or anything?

> *No answer as she exits.* DEL *waits until* REESA *has left.*

DEL: Hey...it was her idea. Bud, you listening to me? [*pause*] You know that expression, "gentleman of leisure"? [*pause*] Huh? [*Pause*] I like that—it fits me don't you think?

> *Pause.* DEL *looks at* BUD, *waiting for answer.* BUD *stares back at him blankly.*

[*definite edge of anger*] Don't pull my chain—OK—Just don't you pull on my chain, huh? [*pause*] Don't pull my fuckin' chain!

> *Pause.* DEL *turns away for a moment—then turns back.*

What's the matter—young thing wants to freak off...

BUD: [*pause*] Yeah?

DEL: Sounds good to me. Right?

BUD: Yeah. [*pause*] Yeah, yeah.

>   REESA *enters with soda. She stops—looking at*
>   BUD. *They stare at each other.*

REESA: All you got is White Rock—

BUD: Yeah.

REESA: I hardly see that brand of soft drink nowadays.

BUD: The store at the corner, it only carries White Rock—
    nothin' else. [*pause*] The owner's got a brother is in
    distribution for White Rock—he's doin' the guy a fa-
    vor. Stock'n all that fuckin' White Rock soda.

>   REESA *takes a sip.*

REESA: Tastes pretty good though, you know.

>   REESA *and* BUD *continue to stare at each other.*
>   DEL *forces a smile but his expression is uncertain.*
>   *Lights fade out.*

SCENE 8

>   *Lights up. Shop, very early morning, almost sun-*
>   *rise.* BUD *stands naked except for bath towel around*
>   *waist. Voice of* REESA *from offstage.*

REESA: [*offstage*] I wasn't any good. [*pause*] It's my fault.

BUD: He found out different than he thought, that's all.

>   *Pause.*

REESA: [*offstage*] I'm sorry...Bud,...I'm sorry.

>   *Silence.*

I couldn't satisfy you both—that's really what's true.

BUD: He didn't like it. It's him.

REESA: [*offstage*] If he was hot then he wouldn't've left.

BUD: That's not it. [*pause*] You're terrific. [*pause*] Reesa?

REESA: [*offstage*] [*pause*] Don't say that. [*pause*] Lie to
   me or some shit.
   Silence.
   He seemed real into it at first.
BUD: Forget it. Forget that, no kidding.
   Long silence.
   You think this is going to work–the plan?
REESA: [*offstage*] Del thinks so.
BUD: What do you think?
REESA: [*offstage*] How should I know?
   Pause.
BUD: You know this isn't the first one we've done.
REESA: [*offstage*] I know it.
BUD: Oh...well, that's right. It's not the first. [*pause*] Del
   tell you?
REESA: [*offstage*] Del said you guys had done a bunch
   of holdups–movie theaters, liquor stores, photomats.
BUD: That's true. We've done that.
   Pause.
REESA: [*offstage*] What's wrong? I won't tell anyone.
   [*pause*] Don't you want to do this one?
BUD: I want to.
REESA: [*offstage*] I'm the one you take the money from.
   That's what makes it so easy Del says.
BUD: Del says that?
REESA: [*offstage*] Yeah.
   Silence.
   Bud?
   Silence. BUD *stands smoking, expressionless.*
   [*louder*] Hey Bud...? [*pause*]
   Silence.

[*offstage*] Bud?! [*pause*] You know Del's only my half brother—step half brother? I don't want you to think something weird.

Silence.

Bud? [*pause*] Was I really terrific—do you think?

BUD *takes off towel and starts to dress—puts on pants, t-shirt, thongs. He exits out rear.*

I'm almost done in here—[*pause*] Sorry I took so long. [*pause*] Bud? [pause] Don't worry about this one...Del says it's cinch domino...a piece of cake.

Pause.

Lights fade out.

SCENE 9

*Lights up. Beachfront edge of stage, night. Actors look out at ocean-audience—*DEL *and* FELIX, *both squatting, drinking from pint bottle in brown paper bag. Both in jacket and knit caps to keep warm. Both are somewhat drunk,* FELIX *more so.*

DEL: ...At that time, that's a fact, [*short pause*]...at that time—you didn't have your "professional" [*says word with disgust*], your "contests." Oh maybe an odd event here and there—but there was no money to speak of—I'm talking here about prize money—like today, thousands of dollars—double figures, for surfing—*surfing!*

Pause. Both men take drink from bottle in bag.

These guys now—they surf, it's the money—the job—they're "professionals" [*again the word is said with disgust*]—not that some aren't good—you know, because that wouldn't be true—no, there are guys today, they're fuckin' awesome—no question there—monsters—fifteen year old kids—monsters—monsters!

Pause. More drinks from bottle.

But underneath that—dig this, Felix, underneath it, what've they got? [*pause*] I don't know because I mean I look—I really look hard for it—trying to see what's going on in this scene—the new thing—and I don't find anything...I don't.

FELIX: [*pause*] Money! Huh?! Money!

DEL: OK—you hit it on the nose—that's right, which is what I'm trying to say—exactly—money. [*pause*] And that's not what it's all about. Money—money is not what it's all about.

FELIX: Money.

DEL: There will come a time—and I know you know what I'm talking about, there will come a time for these kids...you know this right?

FELIX: Absolutely.

DEL: There will come a time—maybe when they get to be our age—maybe then, maybe sooner, could be?—I'm not a philosopher—every man is different—from a different home, different family, and these things make a difference—so, all I'm saying is a day will come—and the money won't be there—new guys comin' up will be winning the money—and that's when—if I'm correct—I don't know—that is when they will wonder what's underneath—but there won't be anything.

Silence.

FELIX: When you get older—you can see these things.

DEL: OK. Looking back at things, you can see. Why?

'Cause you're older. What do kids know…Huh? Am I right?

FELIX: You don't know how to deal with things, not at the time—when you're a kid.

DEL: Let me say this…Bud! [*pause*] This is another matter…But Bud, they would line up on the beach—Felix—say twenty, thirty people—to watch Bud out in that water…Cut back! This was a power cut back—I'm talking nineteen-sixty-nine—you heard of the winter of sixty-nine…

> DEL *stops suddenly and stands up.* FELIX *looks up, bewildered.* DEL *swears under his breath and walks off a couple steps. Silence.*

FELIX: Me and Sherry—excuse me for, you know, but I want to illustrate a point—we didn't know how to deal with things—we were kids.

DEL: I used to watch him.

> *Pause.*

I grew up here—beach town, which stinks. We both grew up in this exact neighborhood.

> *Pause.*

I knew him—not very well—but like I'd see him…of course, later…later…[*softer, trailing off*]…later…

> *Lights fade across to* JILL *and* BUD.

SCENE 10

> *Lights up. Beach, night.* BUD *and* JILL—*he spreads out blanket for them to sit on. Both wear jackets—* JILL *also wears scarf wrapped around her neck.* JILL *sits on blanket.* BUD *sits—then almost immediately*

stands back up. JILL *looks up at him—a little bewildered—also rigid—with hostile attitude. Pause.*

BUD: I don't come here very much.

Pause. Looking at each other.

Not this beach. [*pause*] I don't get to the beach much these days—anymore—[*pause*] This beach is ruined. It's been ruined anyway.

Silence. BUD *looks into darkness, still standing.* JILL *sits looking down into her lap.*

I can't blame you for how you feel—anybody would feel that way. Feel the same way you do.

Pause.

JILL: I don't come to the beach during the day—I stopped going out in the sun—unless I put on a lot of sunscreen. [*pause*] I only stopped two weeks ago after I read this article.

BUD: I believe—if you really put all your energy into it—nothing else—that you can make money. This isn't just some stupid talk—I'm not just sayin' stuff. I think if that's all you do—if all your energy goes into making money—for a whole year—you could make a lot.

Silence.

I wanted to tell you I know. I can't explain all this—but you see the point I'm making, right?

JILL: Yes.

Pause.

BUD: This beach is ruined now.

He squats down close to her.

I'm not making that up am I?

JILL: No, you're not. They've ruined this beach.

BUD: It's a fuckin' shame too. It's awful—what they did, awful.

> *Pause.* BUD *staring directly at* JILL.

My mother, my uncle, they can fuck themselves. I'm a man. Where do they come off…coming to me with their "join the office" crap—Uncle Wes offers me a start, he says, "a start in the middle"—what's that mean? Jesus.

> *Silence.* BUD *stands.*

"Not right now," I said, "Uncle Wes." You know what I'm talking about?!

JILL: Your Dad's office.

BUD: My Dad's office—he acts like it's his now—I should have told him, this is my Dad's office, asshole—this is my Dad's office so don't give me any shit. Give me shit in my own father's office.

JILL: He's got no right.

BUD: Coming up to me with his pussy suggestions. Has his hair cut like a marine. My mother telling me that Wes is getting old. So what?! So what!! [*nearly screaming now*] So what!! So what!!

> BUD *turns away and walks a couple steps up stage—partially in shadows. After a moment* JILL *stands—steps off blanket.*

JILL: I think it's time we left—I'd like to go back to my apartment.

> *Silence.*

Will you take me back now, Bud?

> BUD *turns around and steps over next to* JILL.

BUD: You don't want to hear, ahm…about…ah…about what I figured out?

Silence. JILL *picks up blanket and starts to fold it.*

You don't have to fold it.

JILL: OK.

Lights out.

SCENE 11

Lights up. Shop, late afternoon. FELIX *on floor, half lying, and very drunk.*

FELIX: [*slurred*] Sherry! [*pause*] Sherry?

He struggles to sit up. Pause.

Sugar?...Honey...

He finally sits up.

SHERRY: Will you eat something?

FELIX: Believe me...Will you?

SHERRY: If I make you something...I don't know what's here—if they got anything.

FELIX: Well they got cocaine...and eskatrol...Huh?... Sherry, and what else?

SHERRY: I'll take you to my apartment.

FELIX: Oh, not yet...not yet...

SHERRY: What about your job? You lost your job, haven't you?

FELIX: [*pause*] Don't you know? [*pause*] Del and Bud— huh? They're fuckin' rip off artists.

SHERRY: I know.

DEL *enters from outside but* FELIX *and* SHERRY *don't see him.*

FELIX: Big man Bud...and your boy friend—your Del— fuckin' rip offs. I thought they were good people.

DEL: Felix.

FELIX *and* SHERRY *turn around suddenly,* FELIX *clearly alarmed.*

FELIX: Hey boss. [*smiles weakly*]

DEL *walks over and stands looking down at* FELIX.

DEL: You know what? Should I tell him Sherry? How you talk about him?

SHERRY: What?

DEL: What you say about him...[*to* FELIX] Should I tell you what Sherry says about you? Felix? About your "difficulties" in the sack? We had a good laugh over it Felix—she told it all in detail man...

SHERRY: Jesus.

Silence. DEL *doesn't look at* SHERRY, *only at* FELIX.

FELIX: Del...come on man, let's not be like this...Aren't we friends? [*pause*] Del? Aren't we? Friends?

BUD *enters from outside—rear. Everyone turns and looks at him.* DEL *turns back, looking at* FELIX.

DEL: [*quietly, controlled*] You cunt. You fucking cunt.

DEL *turns away. Pause, no one moves.*

FELIX: [*to* DEL] What you sold me, it wasn't any good. You know that?!

BUD *and* DEL *exchange looks.* SHERRY *starts trying to get* FELIX *to his feet...*

BUD: [*to* FELIX] You buy some coke Felix?

SHERRY: [*to* FELIX] Come on...

FELIX: Bud...

FELIX *finally standing. He looks at* BUD.

You shouldn't rip me off...I thought we'd all be friends.

Long silence as BUD *and* FELIX *stare at each other. Finally* SHERRY *yanks* FELIX *off toward exit.* [*over his shoulder*] Rip off artists…

FELIX *and* SHERRY *exit. Pause.*

DEL: Hey…I think we oughta do it—I think we oughta go tonight.

BUD: [*pause*] How many more?

DEL: What are you asking?

BUD: Because this is stupid—Reesa doesn't know jack shit here.

DEL: Is that a question? Is that the kind of question an adult asks?

BUD: I don't know what kind of question it is.

Pause.

DEL: I cannot say how many. I cannot tell you how many.

BUD: You sold Felix some flea powder—what? What was it? It wasn't coke.

DEL: Do you care?

BUD: You think I care?! I don't care about any of it.

DEL: Fuck'em, all of them, all of them!

Pause.

You want to do this tonight?

Pause.

Reesa's made a chart man—it's a lock.

BUD: Reesa is fucked up.

DEL: Bam, bam and we're out of there.

BUD: Reesa is a joke. It's fucked up, fucked up.

DEL: Come on man, let's go. [*pause*] Let's do it.

DEL *puts his arm around* BUD. *They hug. Lights fade out.*

SCENE 12

Lights up. Minutes later. DEL *and* BUD *are getting dressed for robbery.*

DEL: You think I should wear sunglasses?

Pause.

How about those Ray-Bans? And a hat—you think I need a hat? Bud?

BUD: I think you should—if you want one—I think you should wear a hat.

DEL: [*pause*] You trust me? Do you?

BUD: I trust you—I trust shit—that isn't what's important. No way that matters. Doesn't matter.

DEL *puts on shades.*

DEL: Are we friends? I'm serious now.

BUD: That doesn't matter.

DEL: This doesn't matter either?

BUD: If we split up...Del...where's that leave me?

Long pause.

DEL: [*quiet*] You want a hat for tonight?

BUD: Yeah.

DEL: Here. [*hands him cap*] OK?

BUD: OK [*pause*] Is Reesa ready?

DEL: She's ready—but fuck Reesa—it don't change anything, ready, not ready, it don't change you and me.

Lights fade out.

SCENE 13

Lights up. REESA *standing in fast food uniform, nervous, anxious, visibly shaking.* DEL *standing behind her in hat, sunglasses. Both face audience.*

DEL: Look how you're shaking.

REESA: I'm cold.

DEL: Shaking all over, shaking all over—that's great.

REESA: I forgot my coat.

>*Pause.*

DEL: I wore a hat, and sunglasses, my Ray-Bans... Reesa? Sis?

REESA: I'm trying to stop shaking, Del, but I'm cold.

>DEL *steps forward, closer to* REESA. *Pause.*

DEL: I got my gun, I'm all set—I got my gun, all ready.

REESA: Where's Bud? What's going on?

DEL: Stop that shaking. Stop that fucking shaking.

>*Lights out.*

SCENE 14

>*Lights up. Dim.* JILL *stands against rear wall. Offstage noises, crashes.* BUD *enters, exhausted, weak, pale.*

BUD: Something happened.

JILL: It was on the radio.

>BUD *slowly stumbles forward. Stands near board, trembling.*

BUD: Something.

>*Pause. He looks at surf boards.*

Bud Westly.

>*Pause.* BUD *stumbles to center of room.*

Something has happened.

>*Lights out.*

END

STANDARD OF THE BREED

Standard of the Breed, first presented at the Cast Theatre in Hollywood on August 7, 1988, was directed by the author and had the following cast:

JACK	Bob Glaudini
CASSIE	Diane DeFoe
REESE	Harvey Perr
TEELA	O-Lan Jones
CHUCK	Mick Collins

ACT 1

SCENE

*In dark, sound of large dog barking. Lights up slowly on kennel—*JACK *stands, still in casino uniform, with tie undone and jacket draped over chair.* CASSIE *seated, purse on lap. They listen to barking until it stops.*

CASSIE: It's those birds.

JACK: Crows.

CASSIE: Crows, yes.

> *Silence.*

My, boyfriend, Chuck, he called you.

JACK: Chuck, sure, I know, I... He called yesterday.

CASSIE: He's not feeling well. He stayed at the hotel.

JACK: Did your boyfriend, Chuck? Does Chuck like dogs?

CASSIE: I guess.

JACK: Do you know much about the breed?

CASSIE: Excuse me...I...

JACK: We raise Mastiffs, sometimes referred to as English Mastiffs. [*pause*] How much do you know about Mastiffs?

CASSIE: [*pause*] I'm sorry.

> *Silence. They stare at each other.* CASSIE *stands...*

JACK: Don't go...

CASSIE: Chuck isn't feeling well, he's still at the hotel...

JACK: In Las Vegas?

CASSIE: At the Sands.

JACK: [*nods, smiles*] ...I used to work at the Sands.

> *Pause.* CASSIE *slowly sits.* JACK *pulls up chair and sits facing her. He leans forward, intent.*

Mastiffs are the largest dogs in the world. Great Danes, Irish Wolfhounds, both are a bit taller, but Mastiffs weigh more. Not even Saint Bernards are as big. [*pause*] They're special animals, I believe.

> *Pause.*

Where are you from, Cassie?

CASSIE: I was born in Pennsylvania, right by Penn State.

JACK: [*nods*] Uh huh.

CASSIE: ...But I lived in Tacoma most of the time.

JACK: Washington.

CASSIE: [*nodding–pause*] I live in Los Angeles now.

JACK: With Chuck?

CASSIE: [*nodding*] Not in L.A. exactly. We live in La Habra. Do you know where that is?

> JACK *shakes his head "no."*

Out past Whittier. You know Whittier?

JACK: No.

CASSIE: Richard Nixon was born in Whittier.

> JACK *nods his comprehension.*

We bought a house. [*pause*] Chuck thought a dog would be a good idea... Not, not that La Habra is a bad area, I mean it's not–that's why we decided to buy there, because it's safe.

JACK: [*pause*] Your family, they live in Tacoma?

> CASSIE *looks at him, uneasy, then stands...*

CASSIE: Can I see the puppies?

JACK: You're the first person to see them. You'll have the pick of the litter. Someone is coming later, but... [*pausing, uncertain*] I'm not keeping any, so you'll get any one that you want.

CASSIE: Oh...ah...great. [*smiles, nervous*]

JACK: These dogs...

> CASSIE *sits again.*

...They were used as guards, in the Middle Ages, for the peasants. In England, they kept wolves, boars, anything—they kept the family protected. They were the dogs of the poor.

> CASSIE *nods vaguely.*

I didn't want the dogs of the rich, of the aristocracy. I *chose* Mastiffs, they're common. I chose Mastiffs. [*pause*] Very powerful...

> JACK *stops, he stands slowly and steps closer to*
> CASSIE.

The standard for the breed demands they present a picture of power and strength, of massiveness and dignity. [*pause*] The breeder tries to achieve the standard, which is seen as perfection. The Mastiff must have, despite its size, a gentle nature, and instincts for protection—you try to breed for temperament as well as type. [*pause*] The standard is perfection; every breeder tries to come as close to perfection as he can. [*pause*] All of my money goes into my dogs, all of my time. Everything.

> *Silence. Lights out. In darkness—sound of several dogs barking and yelping.*

SCENE

*Lights up very gradually—we see a bed, pulled
down out of a wall.* CASSIE *asleep. The door to
front yard opens—we make out a figure, a man.*

REESE: Jack?

He enters. CASSIE *turns over, then hears sound
of someone in room and sits up—scared.*

CASSIE: Who is it?

REESE: Shit...it's Reese.

REESE *looks around, he walks over to lamp next
to bed and turns it on.* CASSIE *sits up in bed, she is
in nightgown.*

[*smiles widely*] Hi.

CASSIE *stares at him, frightened.*

Jack around?

CASSIE: I...

She looks around.

REESE: Frightened?

CASSIE: Who are you?

REESE: Jack's boss.

REESE *pulls up chair and sits next to bed, facing*
CASSIE.

Jack's a dealer at the casino. You been to the casino?

CASSIE: I...

She can't answer, sitting instead, shaking.

REESE: [*smiles*] I got here late. You Jack's girlfriend?

CASSIE: No.

REESE: No? I got *my* girlfriend out in the car. [*pause*]
Teela. We came to buy a dog.

They stare at each other.

Maybe Jack's outside. What do you think?

CASSIE: I suppose.

> CASSIE *gets out of bed, trying to keep covered. She starts pulling on her sweater. She looks over at Reese watching her.*

I've got to go.

REESE: Let's find Jack, OK?

> REESE *stands. He watches as* CASSIE *tries to pull on some pants and still keep herself covered with the sheet.*

CASSIE: Don't watch me.

REESE: What are you doin' here?

CASSIE: [*angry, louder*] Quit staring.

> REESE *smiles. Silence.*

Jack let me sleep here.

REESE: Nice guy, Jack.

> CASSIE *is dressed, she puts down the sheet.*

CASSIE: I left my boyfriend. Jack said I could sleep here. That's all.

REESE: Where's your boyfriend?

CASSIE: [*pause*] I don't know exactly.

REESE: [*pause*] You know Jack well?

> CASSIE *sits, on the verge of crying.*

CASSIE: No, I don't know Jack at all.

REESE: Jack loves dogs, he's real into dogs.

CASSIE: Yeah, I bought one of the dogs.

REESE: Yeah?

> *They look at each other.*

CASSIE: Why are you lookin' at me so hard?

REESE: You're what, twenty-two, twenty-three?

CASSIE: Twenty-three.

REESE: Your boyfriend know you're here?

CASSIE: I doubt it.

> REESE *slowly sits back down. Pause.*

Don't you think you better go get your girlfriend?

> REESE *looks at floor, says nothing.*

I just couldn't go back to the hotel, I couldn't do it. [*pause*] Jack is a nice man, don't you think?

REESE: Jack...yeah, Jack is a prince.

> *They stare at each other.*

CASSIE: He slept out back, I mean, he let me alone here, let me have the bed.

REESE: That was very nice of him.

CASSIE: You think I'm ridiculous, huh?

REESE: [*quietly*] No.

CASSIE: I married Chuck, I believe in being married. I just couldn't go back–that doesn't make me a bad person.

REESE: I never said you were a bad person.

CASSIE: That's my car out front, I...,[*hesitates*]

REESE: What are you gonna do now?

CASSIE: I'll go somewhere.

REESE: [*nodding*] OK.

CASSIE: I have the car, not Chuck. I can go where I want, I have a little money.

REESE: You been in Las Vegas–you and Chuck?

CASSIE: Chuck had a two-week vacation, he wanted to go to Vegas. He said we could come out here to buy a dog, too.

REESE: I work at the casino in Ely–

> *Silence.* REESE *stands.* CASSIE *watching him, she looks a little frightened.*

I'm going away, too. [*pause*] I'm going to Los Angeles.

CASSIE: I live in L.A., well, in La Habra, that's near L.A.

REESE: Is it?! Well, that's where I'm going.

CASSIE: You shouldn't leave your girlfriend in the car.

REESE: [*pause*] I'm forty-six and I'm going to pull up and go to Southern California. What do you think of that?!

CASSIE: [*nervous—pause*] You should see my puppy, I'm naming him Aaron—it's a name I like from the Bible.

> REESE *looks at her but says nothing.*

You want to see him?

> REESE *says nothing.*

[*becoming very anxious*] Come on, please.

> REESE *says nothing.*

He's beautiful, he's light brown, fawn—Jack said he was a silver fawn—isn't that beautiful sounding?

> REESE *turns away, he walks to rear door and opens it. It's dark out.*

What time is it?

> REESE *turns back toward her...*

REESE: About three, three-thirty.

> *They stare at each other.*

CASSIE: Be nice to me, would you, please.

REESE: I'm always nice.

> *Silence.* REESE *pulls up chair and sits. Lights cigarette.*

I used to own a motel, in Riviera Beach—Florida. [*pause*] There was a man there, he was from the same town in Oklahoma as my mother. Turned out he wasn't a very nice man—he abducted a girl from the convenience mart down the block. He brought her to the motel. It ended with the police storming the

room, number eleven—they shot him. I had to testify
and go through a whole lot of shit. I sold the place
then, which was all right, I didn't like Riviera Beach
much anyway.

CASSIE *sits listening.*

CASSIE: What happened to the girl?

REESE: I don't know. She moved away. [*shrugs*] I don't
know.

CASSIE: Why'd you come out here so late?

REESE: [*weary*] I don't know that either.

*The front door opens tentatively—*TEELA *sticks
her head in...*

Come on in, baby.

TEELA *enters, wearing low-cut evening dress.*

CASSIE: Hi.

TEELA *stares at her a moment.*

TEELA: Hi.

TEELA *looks around.*

Where's Jack?

REESE: Out back.

REESE *and* TEELA *stare at each other.* REESE
turns to CASSIE...

We got laid off tonight, me and Teela. We both got
shit-canned—both of us.

Silence. TEELA *wearily goes to chair and sits.
Lights fade out.*

SCENE

Lights up—spot on JACK, *seated on stool, rear area
of kennel.* REESE *kneels next to him.*

REESE: They only want girls—new places, especially in Vegas—they want girls if they can find 'em.

> *Silence.* REESE *inches closer...*

Teela wants to go to L.A. [*pause*] What do I do, Jack—tell me.

JACK: I lived in L.A. once. [*pause*] I lived there seven years—I was living with this woman, Margaret—for three years, she lived in Long Beach.

REESE: Teela, she wants me to go—what am I gonna do, Jack, you tell me.

> JACK *looks at him.*

Smells like the monkey cage at the zoo in here. It always smell this way?

JACK: I don't smell it.

> REESE *nods. Silence.*

REESE: I'm not broke, you know I'm not broke.

JACK: Right.

REESE: I got the Cadillac, I still got that.

> REESE *takes handkerchief and mops his brow.*

Five AM and, what, ninety degrees? Maybe it's a good thing, go to L.A.—huh? Lay on the beach, get tan.

> JACK *turns and looks at him.*

JACK: What do you want, Reese?

> REESE *stands.*

REESE: I want comfort, Jack, comfort.

> JACK *suddenly takes a deep gasp of air, he puts his hand to forehead, leaning far forward.* REESE *looks at him...*

Jack... you OK?

> JACK *nods without looking up.*

I didn't mean to come out here so late, I wasn't thinking, you know—me and Teela went 'n had a few
drinks—after they told us—we went over to Bunyons,
then that other place.

He stares down at JACK...

You all right, Jack?

JACK *slowly straightens up...*

JACK: I haven't been feeling well, I can't sleep.

REESE *stands, says nothing.*

You want to see the dogs?

JACK *stands...*

They're exceptional, a beautiful litter, just beautiful.

They stare at each other.

They're very big, noble—these are the best pups I've
produced, the best, these pups stand up against anyone, anywhere. I love this litter, I love them.

JACK *stops, a little short of breath—not feeling
well.*

When I was in Long Beach I was living in this apartment and Margaret was supporting the both of us.
Do you know what happened to Margaret? [*pause*]
Margaret left one day for New Orleans, she went to
her sister's house in fucking New Orleans. She took
the car, which was my car, and she drove. And I called
her sister, I called every day—but she never talked to
me, so I don't know... [*long pause*] I don't recall much
of L.A., I don't recall a whole lot about that period of
my life, I don't care about it—I'm not interested at all,
I'm not concerned, it doesn't matter to me, it's part of
the past, someone else, somewhere else. I never think

about it, about the person I was—I never give it a moment's thought.

> JACK *is wheezing a little and sits down.*

REESE: Who is this girl inside, Jack?

> JACK *stares at ground. Silence.*

Cassie? Who is this girl, this Cassie?

JACK: She just left her husband, left him asleep at the Sands. I don't know him, never met him. She left him though, asleep in bed—left him there—dreaming— Huh? Dreaming in room 418, the Sands, Las Vegas.

> *Lights fade out.*
>
> *In darkness: sound of a woman* (TEELA) *singing a capella—Bill Monroe's "What a Wonderful Life."*

SCENE

> *Lights up slowly on house—through window we see it is light out.* TEELA *standing in center of room, eyes closed, finishing last chorus.* CASSIE *sits watching.*

CASSIE: I love that so much.

> CASSIE *claps a couple times.* TEELA *looks at her.*

Do you sing? I mean, are you a professional singer?

TEELA: Yeah.

> TEELA *turns away, pacing the room slowly. Silence.*

CASSIE: That was a beautiful song.

> TEELA *stops—looks at* CASSIE...

TEELA: Yeah. Yeah, it is.

CASSIE: Yeah. I think it is, definitely.

TEELA: We have to wait until this evening to get our

final pay checks. Now, now they were *supposed* to give 'em to us when they fired us but Eddie—he said no, we weren't fired, we were being let go and that is different.

CASSIE *nods vaguely, listening.* TEELA *sits.*

How old do you think I am?

CASSIE: Oh, god, I don't...

TEELA: [*a little harsh*] Come on—guess.

CASSIE: I'm real bad with how old people are.

They stare at each other, CASSIE *seemingly unnerved.*

You look so good—so, looking so good I would say— I would guess, I would guess, oh, thirty, thirty-one?

TEELA *stares at her, saying nothing. She finally stands, taking pack of cigarettes out of pocket and lighting one.*

TEELA: This evening we'll go get our checks—and then we're gonna drive to Los Angeles. [*pause*] Last time I was in Los Angeles, I went to the car show, with my brother Donald—I was fifteen.

She looks at CASSIE...

That's how long it's been. Why's it taken me twenty years or so to get back? Over twenty years. I'd get someplace—places I didn't want to be, and I just couldn't get out of those places.

Silence. TEELA *paces.*

That makes you feel you've wasted something. I'm not ignorant—I'm not really, I don't *believe* something is going to happen—you know—like something ridiculous—but I intend to go, I don't plan on making believe but I intend to go and take my shot. I've a right to take my shot, even though, even though, you know, it won't amount to anything. It won't change anything.

  TEELA *stops, puffing intently on cigarette.* CASSIE *looks away, nervous, uncomfortable.*

I have a lovely voice.

CASSIE: You do, you have a beautiful singing voice.

  TEELA *nods.*

TEELA: Well, we'll get our checks, and we'll get on our way.

CASSIE: Reese seems very nice.

TEELA: Reese is nice, yes, you could probably say he's a nice guy. [*pause*] Reese has a way of landing on his feet—he can carve himself a niche, he can go somewhere, someplace, a new place, and he can carve himself a little niche—find the angle, Reese knows the angles—Reese can spot the opportunity, his experience has taught him to recognize opportunity when he trips on it. I'm not like that, I just trip—I never seem to know what's going on till it's much later. Some people are like that—that's just how it is. I don't know the score until the teams are on their way to the next game. Reese has cunning, you look at his face, he has an expression, like an animal or like a shark—whatever it is, it's a matter of self-preservation, with him, what we're looking at is self-preservation.

  Pause.

CASSIE: Where you gonna stay in Los Angeles?

TEELA: I don't know. The beach I guess, I'd like to get someplace where I could walk to the beach. [*pause*] I wonder what would've happened if, say, if I was going and I was ten years younger.

They stare at each other. Pause.

Because you can't expect much if you're not real young. Unless you're still young, what people think of as young—you're going to have to be realistic.

CASSIE: I don't know [*pause*]—I don't have much experience. I know *you* do, and I'd like to feel I could have "experience" like that. [*pause*] I'm really scared...

> CASSIE *is close to tears, and looks imploringly at* TEELA, *who turns away. Silence.*

Chuck, when I met him—I worked at the Taco Tico near the campus and he'd come in and kept asking for a date...

> TEELA *turns and looks at her.*

TEELA: What kind of work does Chuck do?

CASSIE: Oh, he, he's in the construction business— [*pause*] Chuck is older than me—but, then, I think that that is OK—don't you?

TEELA: Sure.

CASSIE: Chuck—I didn't know much about him when we met. I just wanted to get out of Tacoma, and Los Angeles sounded fine, really fine.

TEELA: Well—now we're at Jack Taylor's house, six thirty, outside Ely...

CASSIE: Why'd you come here?

> TEELA *stares at her, turns away.*

Do you know Jack pretty well?

> TEELA *turns back to her...*

TEELA: Do I know Jack? No. I hardly know him at all. He deals blackjack, at the casino.

CASSIE: Do you sing there?

TEELA: No, honey—I serve cocktails.

CASSIE: So Jack is a friend of Reese's?

> TEELA *stares at her. Pause.*

TEELA: Yeah, yeah, that's right, that's about it.

CASSIE: Have you seen Jack's dogs? They're incredible—
I bought one of the puppies.

TEELA: Isn't that nice.

CASSIE: I call him Aaron.

> TEELA *nods vaguely. Silence.*

Are you mad at me?

TEELA: I'm just not real interested in dogs—Jack's dogs,
anybody's. [*pause*] When you plan on leaving?

CASSIE: I...I'm not definite—I suppose this morning. I'm
afraid Chuck is gonna find me.

TEELA: You think Chuck will come out here? He knows
about Jack's kennel?

CASSIE: Oh yeah, he's talked with Jack on the phone.

> TEELA *turns away. She waits a moment then goes
> to the door and opens it.*

TEELA: [*yelling*] Reese?

> *No answer. She suddenly shuts the door and turns
> back to* CASSIE.

Does Chuck, does he make good money?

CASSIE: I don't know—I guess so.

> TEELA *wearily sits. Silence.* CASSIE *smiles ten-
> tatively at her.*

Jack seems really nice, quiet.

> *Pause.*

TEELA: My father was a little like Jack—kept to himself—but he had a drug problem and he beat my mom.

[*pause*] I see all these people, families, come to the casino, or in Vegas—these real American families, and I see the parents are drunk—always fighting, and they hate each other...deep down, they hate each other and you can see their kids, they hate the kids—they don't know, maybe, that they hate them, like they know they hate each other, but if you look at these crazy little fuckers, if you just look at the kids, you know there is something wrong.

TEELA *stares at* CASSIE...

So we got all these nuts kids, raised by nuts, and I wonder how it all keeps going... Do you see? How does the paper get delivered and so on—[*pause*] You got any kids?

CASSIE: [*shaking head "no"*] No.

TEELA: I had two—I wasn't married, I had this boyfriend. [*pause*] But they're grown and gone—I never hear from them, from my kids, never. [*pause*] It's all so fucking sick, isn't it?

CASSIE: I don't know.

TEELA: [*pause*] If Reese ever hit me I'd cut his fucking throat.

Long silence. Lights fade out.

SCENE

Lights up slowly: JACK *making coffee in small kitchenette to side of room. Bed in back wall.* CASSIE *sits at table as does* TEELA. REESE *paces, smoking.*

REESE: [*to everyone in general*] Anything you want to know about dogs—Jack can tell you—I mean, this guy

was the worst blackjack dealer in Nevada—but, hey—
ask him about dogs—

> REESE *snaps his finger.* JACK *stares at him silently.*

The sound of barking dogs—I never cared for that
sound. It always made my flesh creep—my bones hurt,
a dog barks and I think, how can I kill it. [*laughs*] [*to*
JACK] Just kidding, Jack. [*to* CASSIE] Jack's not a great
kidder, not if we're talkin' dogs. [*laughs*]

> JACK *takes cups of coffee to* CASSIE *and* TEELA.

What about me, Jack?

> JACK *turns away, goes back to kitchenette and
brings* REESE *a cup as* REESE *continues…*

Jack knows I love him, Jack knows I'm the reason
they didn't fire him, he knows I covered his ass many
a time.

> JACK *hands him cup, then turns away, goes back
to kitchenette.*

[*to* CASSIE] Sweetie, let's talk about you—

> REESE *pulls up stool to sit close to her…*

Listening to all our problems—and you sittin'—with
real problems of your own. Now—this guy Chuck—
you sure you don't want to go on back to Vegas, the
guy must be worried—probably called the cops by
now, filed a missing persons report.

CASSIE: I don't know what to do.

REESE: No, no this kind of matter, between people—
people who are close, people who have shared intimacy—it's not an easy thing to, to ah…analyze—I
know this. It puts you between the ol' rock and hard

place—it's a real tough decision—[*pause*] What are you gonna do if you leave Chuckie, huh? You want to go back to mom and dad, is this what you want?

    REESE *looks at her, waiting for answer...*

CASSIE: I don't... I think, Chuck, he's gonna be mad.

    CASSIE *and* REESE *stare at each other*—REESE *then breaks into wide grin.*

REESE: Sheeit—uncle Reese, he'll make sure old Chuck keeps it in check. OK?! Huh?!

    TEELA *gets up, vaguely disgusted. She crosses room, stops... Everyone watches her except* REESE, *who watches* CASSIE.

TEELA: Lots of fun shit here, huh?

    Turns to REESE...

You think? Reese? Lots of fun shit—party time at Jack Taylor's kennel?!!

    REESE *looks back at* CASSIE, *then back to* TEELA...

REESE: [*to* TEELA] Smells like the monkey cage—but otherwise, I like it. [*to* JACK] I like Jack, too—

    REESE *walks over to* JACK, *who sits silently on stool.* REESE *puts his arm around him.*

[*to* JACK] You know I like you, right? [*pause*] Jack?

JACK: Right.

    REESE *pats him on back, smiles...*

REESE: Right—my man, Jack—Jack, my main man—right Hoss?! [*laughs*] Shit yes.

    REESE *moves away from* JACK...

Well, yeah, things are a little slow here at that—[*to* JACK] You got a CD, Jack?

JACK: What?

REESE: I got some disks in the car—you got a CD player?

JACK: [*confused*] No...ah...uh uh. [*pause*] I got a record player out back.

REESE: Well, maybe we'll get Teela to sing for us—[*to TEELA*] You know Jack's a big fan of yours.

TEELA: [*weary*] Please shut up.

> TEELA *gets up, goes out back door.* REESE *turns his attention back to* CASSIE.

REESE: I bet Chuck, he's gonna be callin' here today.

CASSIE: Yeah.

REESE: I'd like to meet Chuck. You think me and Chuck, we'd hit it off?

> CASSIE *looks over at* JACK, *then back to* REESE.

CASSIE: Is it always this hot here?

REESE: Mostly, yeah.

CASSIE: I feel like we're imposing on Jack.

REESE: Jack don't mind—he's a pay me no mind kind of guy—you know what I mean?

> *Silence.*

You want to know something.

> CASSIE *stares at him, says nothing.*

[*with edge*] Do you?

> *Silence.*

Shit—I'll tell you—this is the thing; I don't *want* to go to L.A.

> REESE *hunches over close to* CASSIE...

So, you ask, why am I going? Huh? Well, I'll tell you— maybe I'm not.

> REESE *straightens up.*

[*to* JACK] No CD, huh? Damn. [*pause*] Jack—you know, I mean, if they let me go, then I'd say there's not

much chance for you—that's America, though, huh—
Job security. [*pause*] What the fuck you do all day,
Jack—no TV, no nothin'.

    JACK *stands.*

JACK: I got to feed the dogs.

REESE: Right—right—good idea.

    JACK *strolls outside.*

CASSIE: You really think I should call Chuck?

REESE: [*pause*] Yeah. [*pause*] Fuck yes, call the fool.

    REESE *walks away, lights cigarette.* CASSIE *stares
    at him.*

CASSIE: It's so hot.

    Pause.

Why's anybody want to live here?

REESE: Baby, I don't know. [*pause*] But there's a reason,
I know that. It's just I ain't found that reason yet.

    CASSIE *nods vaguely. Lights fade out.*
    In dark: sound of TEELA *singing.*

SCENE

    Lights up slowly on TEELA *in stage right pool of
    light as she finishes singing.* CASSIE *stands in stage
    left light, watching* JACK, *kneeling with buckets of
    offal, tripe, etc. for dogs. This is outside, so light is
    hot and white.* CASSIE *inches closer to* JACK…

JACK: This is meat scraps, tripe, kidney, chicken meal—
hearts, lungs, everything.

    They look at each other.

CASSIE: I called Chuck and he's gonna take a cab and
meet me here tonight. [*pause*] Do you mind, you
know, if I stay here today.

JACK *looks at her, then returns attention to dog food.*

JACK: [*long pause*] You should feed your puppy three times a day—feed him this way—feed him flesh—blood—warm the blood...and throw in some rice if you want, other things.

Silence.

CASSIE: I guess all of you are out of work, huh?

Silence.

I'm sorry.

JACK: I'll have to let the dogs go. I got seven adult dogs—I'll have to let 'em go. [*pause*] I believed, at one time that the dogs would go forever—I felt their strength lasting long after I was gone... That's what I imagined... Generation after generation, perfecting the breed, all from my original stock—that's like a legacy.

JACK *stands, picks up buckets.*

But nothing lasts—you don't get anything to last anymore. Not in your life—not in your dreams. Everything just winds down, doesn't it?! [*pause*] I can't imagine anymore, I can't see at night, when I close my eyes, I don't see the things I used to see, ten, fifteen years ago... [*pause*] When I was a boy I dreamed many things... And none of them happened, I wanted, I remember wanting to be a northwest mounted policeman... [*pause*]

Silence. He drops one of the buckets—it spills. Both of them look at it. Lights fade out.

ACT 2

In dark: sound of "Hot Rod Lincoln" plays—a scratchy old 45. Lights come up gradually to reveal JACK *seated in back, smoking cigarette, bottle of old Kessler on ground next to him. It is twilight. Shadows of big dog appear intermittently, flickering across rear scrim. As song is ending, lights are about full—and* JACK *picks up arm of his ancient record player and puts it back at start of record and we again hear "Hot Rod Lincoln" as* JACK *continues to sit passively. Lights now up slowly at other end of stage to reveal* CHUCK *standing, his appearance disheveled—two or three day growth of beard, clothes soiled, etc. His left coat sleeve is folded up at shoulder—his left arm amputated. He steps into house, sound of song gradually lowers to background sound.* CHUCK *stands in center of very dark room, only small spot on his face—suddenly lights come on full and we see* REESE *and* TEELA *seated in chairs.* CHUCK *and* REESE *look at each other and suddenly* REESE *is on his feet...*

REESE: Well—let's see now, you look like you might be Chuck.

      CHUCK *stares at him sourly*

Cassie went for a drive, I believe. [*turns to* TEELA] Yes? Cass went driving?

TEELA *looks at him without responding.*
Out in the desert, her and the puppy—Aaron she named it—Cassie took Aaron out into the empty wastes of south central Nevada.

REESE *smiles at* CHUCK, *who remains expressionless.*
Sit down, here...

REESE *pulls up his chair and* CHUCK *sits.*
Long cab ride—from Vegas.

CHUCK: I didn't take no cab. [*pause*] Got a ride with a Hormel meat truck.

REESE: Hmmm.

TEELA *stands.*

CHUCK: Anyone got a cigarette?

TEELA: Yeah.

TEELA *gives him cigarette. Lights it for him.*
Would you like some coffee, we got instant coffee—

CHUCK *ignores her.* TEELA *turns away, looks at* REESE, *then walks out back. Lights dim on* REESE *and* CHUCK—*and come up on* TEELA *in back with* JACK. *After a moment's silence,* TEELA *steps over closer to* JACK...
You like it here, Jack? Do you really like it?

JACK: Here—in back? Do you mean in back, or here at the kennel—or, just Nevada, just the desert?

TEELA: [*shrugs*] The desert.

JACK: I didn't always live here.

TEELA *stands, waiting for more.* JACK *takes 45 of "Hot Rod Lincoln" off of turntable and puts on Hank Snow's "I've Been Everywhere." He turns it up loud as lights fade out.*

SCENE
Music fades gradually in dark. Lights up on REESE *and* CHUCK *seated together. Each has a can of beer.*

REESE: You ever feel disappointed? [*pause*] OK, what I'm asking is, does your life, what you do—does it seem disappointing?

CHUCK: I can't say. I don't look on it like that.

REESE: [*pause*] You're a big man—physically.
Silence.

I feel disappointed. [*pause*] I'm sure Cassie will be back any time now.
REESE *stands, checks his watch.*

Guess I can go get my check—with Teela, we can go get our checks. [*pause*] I never went to school, my father took me around with him. He was a salesman, and a great card player. I learned gaming, by the time I was fifteen I knew it all, all the odds—craps, poker, even stuff like baccarat—I knew it.

CHUCK: I play craps, that's what I do.
REESE *stares at him. Lights fade out on* CHUCK *and* REESE *while coming up on* TEELA *and* JACK, *both kneeling, looking out over the desert...*

TEELA: I've been in Nevada for fifteen years. [*pause*] It feels like an interruption—you know?! [*pause*] When I left Chicago, maybe it was already too late.
She looks at JACK, *waiting for an answer.* JACK *says nothing.*

I just got stuck somehow—first with Donald, then with

Jeff—you remember him—Jeff Markham?—Then Reese.
I just can't stand being alone.
> *Pause.* TEELA *stands...*

You ought to see him Jack—he's only got one arm.
> *Silence.*

Jack? [*pause*] Why don't you come on inside... We're
gonna leave pretty soon...
> JACK *stands, they look at each other...*

[*quietly*] Here... Give me a hug. [*pause*] Will you?
> *She steps over close to* JACK *and puts her arms
> around him. After a moment,* JACK *slowly puts his
> arms around her. In distance, sound of several dogs
> barking and howling. Lights fade out.*

SCENE
> *Lights up slowly on house:* REESE *stands to one
> side.* CHUCK *is seated.* TEELA *sits in corner and*
> JACK *stands by kitchenette.*

REESE: What is it to L.A.? Three hours? I guess more
like four, four and a half.
> REESE *paces back and forth.*

Not really so far, is it?
> *Silence.*

CHUCK: Anyone got another cigarette?
> TEELA *gets up and hands* CHUCK *a cigarette,
> then lights it for him.*

TEELA: [*to* CHUCK] She'll be back.
REESE: Yeah—she just got caught up in that desert—in
drivin' the desert.
> CHUCK *looks at* REESE.

TEELA: [*to* REESE] It's after nine—it's time to get our checks.

    REESE *looks at her.*

REESE: Yeah, sure. Let's go see Eddie—let's go get our checks.

    REESE *takes his car keys out of his pocket. He and* TEELA *stare at each other.*

TEELA: You go, baby, I'll wait here. [*pause*] I don't want to see Eddie.

REESE: [*pause*] Yeah, yeah, OK.

    REESE *looks around room at everyone—as though he wants to say something—but he doesn't. He turns and looks long at* TEELA, *then turns and exits. Silence.* CHUCK *flicks cigarette against far wall.*

CHUCK: [*to* JACK] You got another beer in there?

    JACK *brings him a beer—opening it as he walks to* CHUCK...

You know—maybe she won't be coming back. [*pause*] Maybe I'll just sit here, hour after mother fuckin' hour—maybe that's how it's goin' to be.

    JACK *stares at him, then turns away and stands by exit.*

What do you do?

TEELA: I worked at the casino, in Ely.

    CHUCK *nods vaguely. Silence.*

CHUCK: I'm tired. [*pause*] Who's Eddie?

TEELA: Just this guy.

    TEELA *stands, starts pacing.*

Eddie is a prick.

CHUCK: Can I lay down someplace?

    TEELA *looks over at* JACK.

JACK: This bed pulls down. The bed here in the wall.

> CHUCK *holds a piece of his shirt up to his nose—smelling it. He looks at* TEELA *and then* JACK.

CHUCK: Any hunting here, Jack? Around here?

JACK: No, I don't think so.

> CHUCK *nods. Pause.*

CHUCK: I'm from Washington state, plenty of hunting up there. [*pause*] I'd like to move back there, sometime, I'd like to go back there.

> *Silence.* JACK *wanders out back.*

I'm just gonna lay down for awhile.

> *Silence. Lights fade out. Sound of dogs barking in dark.*

SCENE

> *Spot up slowly on* REESE *standing in rear.* JACK *stands next to side, looking out at desert.*

REESE: There's a fight on tonight...Jack? On ESPN, two middleweights, both unbeaten—should be a good fight.

> REESE *stares at* JACK *for a moment...*

Doesn't hold a lot of interest for you, huh?!—Well, yeah, I can't blame you. [*pause*] But fights—you have to see them in person. It's the smell mostly—it's the smell of the past. The deep past—the smell of fear, of other things, things that nobody wants to keep.

> *Pause.*

I'm your only friend, Jack—your only friend. Do you know that?

> JACK *stares at him—* REESE *becoming more upset...*

Shit—What you gonna do now, Jack? What? Huh? You thought about that? Because I'm gone, I'm gone, Jack.

REESE *gently, but with urgency takes hold of* JACK.

[*quietly*] Tell me something, [*pause*] please.

REESE *lets go, turns away, trying to collect himself.*

There's nobody to tell me what to do—right?!

Silence.

Do you think about it, Jack? About the mistakes in your life?

JACK: Mistakes? No, I don't think about them.

REESE: OK...OK. [*pause*] I'm doing what I know is best for me. [*pause*] I don't like it. It's nothing to like, is it?

JACK: No, I guess it isn't.

REESE: No. [*pause*] There's nothing to like in any of it.

Silence. He turns and abruptly moves off as lights fade out.

SCENE

Spot up slowly on JACK *in rear. He stands, looking out into the darkness. He begins talking before we see who he is talking to.*

JACK: In the Navy, my father saw a man lose a leg. Got it crushed. He said the man was screaming, in great pain—and he was screaming for his mother. A grown man this was—not a kid—and he was laying there, blood everywhere, screaming for his mother.

We now see CASSIE *standing to side, listening. She has coat on.*

I've never seen anything like that. [*pause*] My mother, she said when she was a little girl she was driving cross country with her step-father and they came up on this terrible crash at a railroad crossing—where a train had hit this car. She didn't want to look but her step-dad stopped and made her look—and she said two people had been decapitated.—She said it was the worst thing she ever saw, the very worst.

> *Pause.*

As a little boy, I remember she would never let me look at any kind of accident—she was very—she would really react strongly to any little accident.

CASSIE: Jack?

JACK: [*pause*] Chuck's asleep inside.

CASSIE: [*pause*] I love the dog, Jack—my puppy—Aaron. I love him, I really love him, he's beautiful, really, really, beautiful.

> *They look at each other. Lights fade out as...*

SCENE

> *Lights up slowly on house:* CHUCK *sits on edge of bed, smoking.* TEELA *sits in chair.*

CHUCK: I heard a car... Whose car was that?

TEELA: Cassie.

> CHUCK *nods. Silence.*

CHUCK: I'm a lot older than Cassie.

> *Pause.*

TEELA: I've wanted to go to Los Angeles for years. We don't do what we want, though, we don't do it like that.

> CASSIE *enters slowly from rear. She and* CHUCK *look at each other.* CASSIE *walks over and sits in chair next to the bed. Long silence.*

CASSIE: You should see the dog, Chuck—he's a great dog.

CHUCK: Yeah...sure.

> *Pause.*

CASSIE: You know what I did, when I was out driving? I stopped at a pay phone—at a gas station, to call my sister—then—standing in this phone booth, I remember, I don't have her number—I don't know where she is.

> *Pause.*

Did you sleep?

CHUCK: No, uh, uh.

> CHUCK *covers his face with his hand, his head lowering—trying not to sob. Lights out.*

SCENE

> *In dark, the sound of* CHUCK *singing. "Goodnight, Irene"—lights up gradually as he's almost done—standing in center of room.* TEELA *stands at rear, glass of bourbon in hand.* CASSIE *sits cross-legged on the bed.* JACK *sits in chair.* CHUCK *finishes.— There is an almost empty fifth of Old Granddad on the floor by bed. Everyone has been drinking.*

CHUCK: Greatest song I know—ought to be the national anthem. [*laughs*] A great American song.

> JACK *stands.*

JACK: "Wabash Cannonball."

CHUCK: Wha...?

JACK: Wabash Cannonball"—that's the real national anthem.

> CHUCK *stumbles to bed and sits.*

CHUCK: Shit—

> JACK *steps over near bed...*

JACK: "Wabash Cannonball"—ask anyone—what's the American anthem?—Huh? Ask anyone...

> JACK *turns away in disgust.* CHUCK *leans in close to* CASSIE. *He takes hold of her chin...*

CHUCK: She's somethin'—look at this face.

> CASSIE *gently pulls away.* CHUCK *looks over at* JACK.

[*to* JACK] Any more "Granddad"?

> JACK *ignores him as he makes his way back to chair.* CHUCK *returns attention to* CASSIE.

Why'd you leave me—in Vegas—why'd you leave me there.

> *Silence.*

CASSIE: I don't know, Chuck.

CHUCK: [*quietly*] You don't know?

> CASSIE *shakes her head, "no." Pause.*

I need a shower—

> CHUCK *turns toward* JACK...

Got a shower here?

> JACK *stares at him, silence.* CHUCK *shrugs—turns back to* CASSIE.

You blame me?

CASSIE: For what?

CHUCK: Do you blame me?

CASSIE: No—Chuck...

CHUCK: I don't want you to blame me.

> CASSIE *nods.*

[*getting a little ugly*] I don't want your blame. [*pause*] I can't use it.

> CHUCK *stands, wobbly.*

There's always a lesson—a lesson to be learned. [*pause*]

There are things wrong today, in the world, and because, in our country... We don't teach young people, we, we don't teach the lessons, like who blames who...

Turns attention to CASSIE.

See...see, I don't ask for anything.

CASSIE: [*tenderly*] What's wrong, Chuck?

CASSIE *gets up, touches his chest gently with her hand...*

I don't blame you–I don't know what you mean. [*pause*] What's the matter, honey?

CHUCK *sits–suddenly exhausted. Long silence.*

TEELA: [*to* JACK] Reese has my things. In the trunk, he's got both my suitcases. [*pause*] I wish he'd left them. [*pause*] Reese isn't coming back–which isn't so bad–but he's got all my things.

TEELA *gets up, walks toward rear. As she does,* CHUCK *has stretched out asleep on bed.* TEELA *stares out at desert.*

Lots of space between things. You see things coming out here. [*pause*] It doesn't matter though, how much time you get. It just doesn't matter.

Lights fade out.

SCENE

In dark, sound of wind blowing–lights up slowly on rear: TEELA *and* CASSIE, *both with jackets on.*

TEELA: Gets cold in a hurry, huh.

Silence.

In winter it snows here sometimes–it snowed last

winter. [*pause*] After a point–at some point in your life everything seems about like everything else.

CASSIE: I always felt I was just average. [*pause*] And that seemed OK to me.

TEELA: I guess it is OK.

CASSIE: I don't want to go back, to California. Not with Chuck.

TEELA: Well, maybe it's time to go out in the world.

CASSIE: I'm afraid.

TEELA: That's OK.

CASSIE: I'm afraid that I'll find out that I'm a person who can't be out in the world alone.

> TEELA *says nothing. Silence.*

TEELA: I'm going to California, even without Reese.

> *Silence.*

I'd spend so much time in the casino, even after I got off–I'd watch Reese, who was the pit boss–I'd watch him, or just go play the nickel slots. [*pause*] There is so much time here and so little to do... It's a town waiting, of people waiting. You can drive through here and not remember it. Though, I like driving around at night, when the car felt cold. I like having the heater on, so my feet stayed warm–but you could touch the window glass and feel the cold.

CASSIE: I'm going to leave, I'm going to take the car. [*pause*] It's Chuck's car but I think he won't do anything, you know, he won't call the police or anything.

TEELA: No, I don't think he will.

CASSIE: If you're here, will you tell him, say that he should not call the police on me.

TEELA: He won't do anything. He knows, he's old enough to know how this works. The price of a ten-year old Buick is little enough.

> CASSIE *turns up the collar on her coat. Sound of wind increases. Pause.*

CASSIE: It's the drinking. He doesn't drink all the time. [*pause*] He told me he was married once before, the daughter of a grower out in Bremerton. She couldn't have children I guess, but he never asked me to have children.

> *Pause.*

TEELA: Goodbye, Cassie.

> *Pause.*

CASSIE: Bye.

> TEELA *smiles briefly, then turns away and walks back inside.*
> *Lights fade out.*

SCENE

Sound of dogs barking, more viciously than usual, and louder. Lights up gradually, on small area near the bed. CHUCK *is sprawled out asleep.* TEELA *approaches, takes off coat, then dress, and wearing only a slip she carefully crawls onto bed next to* CHUCK. *Lights dim out on bed...*

SCENE

As lights come up on rear: JACK *seated next to his old record player, which is now closed, unplugged. A couple old 45s on the ground, another broken 45 by his foot.* CASSIE *steps over to him.*

JACK: Hank Snow, I love Hank Snow...Webb Pierce... Ersel Hickey...All those guys.

> JACK *now turns and looks up at her...*

How long you been standing there?

> CASSIE *says nothing, she shivers and pulls her coat tighter around her.*

Takin' Chuck's car? [*pause*] Nice car. [*pause*] I had this car—[*pause*] I had this hot rod—I was a kid, this was when I was a kid... in Las Cruces, I had a genuine hot rod—this is fifty, fifty-one, and I'm sixteen.

> *Pause.* CASSIE *steps closer.*

There was this boy, Red. [*pause*] Red was beautiful— he was a few years older, you know—he was already out of high school and so forth. I just went everywhere Red went—everywhere. Red didn't have a car, so I'd drive. I'd drive wherever he wanted to go. I just wanted to be with him—[*pause*] One time I had gotten some money, I forget where, and I went out and bought Red some clothes—I wanted him to look good. Red could wear clothes, just the way some people can—well, Red could. And he did look good, just real good. [*pause*] I liked doin' things for him. [*pause*] We ran together for almost a whole year.

> JACK *stops, looks down. Silence.*

CASSIE: What happened to Red.

JACK: What? ...he went away with a girl, a Mexican girl. Pretty girl. [*pause*] We'd drive this hill all the time— get drunk, and drive down this long downgrade. I heard later someone died doing the same thing, two high school boys. [*pause*] But that was later.

> *Silence.*

CASSIE: It felt good out there, with the puppy. He was on the front seat next to me.

They look at each other. Silence.

It felt good driving—[*pause*] Now I'm just waiting, a little, just wanting to get it right. Just wanting to leave right, pull out of the driveway here, hear that gravel, and then find the road under my feet, the road under me. [*pause*] Jack?

JACK *says nothing.*

There's a feeling, something about feeling like I'm growing up—like leaving these problems behind, and the lights here just get smaller...and I got my puppy with me—my puppy who I named Aaron—And behind me it all disappears.

Silence.

JACK: Leave it, just leave it behind.

CASSIE *nods, as she slowly backs out. Lights fade out.*

SCENE

Lights up on room: TEELA *seated on bed.* CHUCK *in same clothes as before, stands staring out at rear.*

CHUCK: [*half to himself*] Unemployed now, I guess—back to that.

He turns toward TEELA.

It's almost morning. [*pause*] Mornings, I like morning out here.

TEELA: You got any money left?

CHUCK *sits down, takes out wallet—counts his money. He looks up at* TEELA...

CHUCK: You want to come with me?

TEELA: No, no thanks.

CHUCK: I'm serious, no joking—why don't you come with me, I got nine hundred left, in cash—there's more I could get.

TEELA: I don't think so.

> CHUCK *gets up and comes over to bed. He sits. Silence.*

CHUCK: Cassie was young. I'm not mad.

TEELA: [*gently*] You've no right to be mad.

CHUCK: [*pause*] The guy I got a ride with, the truck driver. He talked to me, about his wife. He said there were things you don't get over—like his wife leaving him, or when his brother went to prison.

> *Pause.*

TEELA: You don't have to go back to Los Angeles.

> *Pause.*

You could just get up and go back to Washington— up to Oregon, or Canada… You could do any of that.

> CHUCK *looks away.*

CHUCK: I'm too old to do anything that way.

> CHUCK *stands…* JACK *enters from rear. He looks at* CHUCK, *then* TEELA, *then walks to kitchenette. He starts to make instant coffee.*

[*to* JACK] I'll be outta here—as soon as it starts to get light.

> JACK *nods. He comes over and stands next to bed. After a beat, he sits.*

JACK: I'm about ready. I'm letting the dogs go, just before sunrise.

> TEELA *stares at him.*

Then I'm goin' to the Greyhound station in Ely and

get a ticket to Sacramento, somewhere—not too big,
but somewhere bigger than here—to a city. [*pause*] I
want to just do as little as I can.

TEELA: You gonna sell the house here?

JACK: Nobody'd buy it. I'll leave that guy, the guy at the
real estate office, I'll leave him the papers—give him
the right to sell it.

TEELA: I'm sorry about your dogs.

JACK: I'm gonna drink—I'm gonna stay drunk, for as long
as I can. I'll spend days talkin' to the old guys on the
steps of the hotel. You've seen those kind of guys,
right? No family, no reason to do anything, just mark-
ing time. I'm gonna find a hotel like that, full of old
guys like that.

> JACK *turns away and carries his cup with him
> to the chair. He sits. Pause.*

They're beautiful dogs, Mastiffs. This kind of dog—
living with these dogs, it changes your life.

> *Silence.* JACK *suddenly throws cup down, break-
> ing it.* TEELA *and* CHUCK *stare at him. Lights out.*

SCENE

> *Sound of wind blowing. Lights up slowly on bed
> as wind fades.* TEELA *sitting up, on edge.* CHUCK
> *seated on other side, resting his back against head-
> board.*

CHUCK: You have any money?

TEELA: [*pause*] No.

> CHUCK *takes out wallet and hands her several
> large bills.* TEELA *takes it.*

CHUCK: That should get you to Los Angeles.

TEELA: I'm not sure now, not sure about going.

> CHUCK *nods vaguely. He leans back.*

I can find work here—but a new place, there's always trouble.

CHUCK: Where you think Reese went?

TEELA: [*shrugs*] East, I guess—that direction.

> CHUCK *moves over closer to her, until they're touching. He buries his head in her shoulder. Silence.*

What's gonna happen to those dogs?

> CHUCK *doesn't answer. Pause.*

I guess they'll die, unless someone finds one of them. [*pause*] Most will die.

> *While they continue—lights come up very slowly, almost imperceptibly on rear—on* JACK. *He is in coat, with several leather leashes over his shoulder, and large metal key ring. Sound of dogs barking intermittently…*

[*quietly*] Would you say I'm average? Chuck?

> CHUCK *lifts his head, leans back a little.*

CHUCK: I don't know.

TEELA: I'd never thought so.

> *Silence. Sound of dogs barking increases.*

CHUCK: Can you sing "Goodnight, Irene"?

> *Pause.*

TEELA: [*gently*] I don't want to sing just now.

> *Lights fade out on them as they continue to increase on* JACK. *On scrim the light of early morning increases subtly—and sound of dogs barking,*

JOHN STEPPLING

fighting, etc., increases dramatically—Shadows of huge [out size] dogs moving behind JACK *can be seen as sound becomes very loud—painfully so.* JACK *sinks to his knees, grabbing his ears to shut out noise. Lights out. Sound of wind in darkness.*

END

MY CRUMMY JOB

My Crummy Job, directed by Diane DeFoe, was performed on December 4 and 5, 1989 at The Taper Too, New Works Festival. The play was produced by the Mark Taper Forum in Los Angeles and had the following cast:

PAIGE	Megan Butler
IKE	Richard Herd
JUNIOR	Rick Dean

Lights up: PAIGE, *mid twenties, sits in chair.* IKE, *mid fifties, stands, both are smoking.*

PAIGE: My shit was shot out—[*pause—takes deep drag on cigarette*] I was about on the street—there were people who helped me—I'm not saying that—these guys, like my brothers—burnt out motherfuckers like they were, but I could've been much worse off. [*pause—takes another long drag on cig*] You think I like that job—I don't like it.

IKE: [*nodding agreement/understanding*] It's a crummy job.

PAIGE: Fifty cents over minimum and tips. And tips aren't shit.

IKE: No, often not.

Pause—IKE *finally pulls up chair and sits.*

I've had this idea—about shoes.

PAIGE: Yeah?

IKE: Because I have access—access, into places—access to people—in wholesale, where I can get samples of Italian shoes, English men's shoes, the best stuff—and we have them copied—and I can set up some deal with Junior's uncle—maybe his store in Tustin—or in San Diego. [*pause*] I can have them copied in Tijuana—cheap—this can be done cheaply.

PAIGE: Sounds like a lot of hassle.

IKE: [*with edge*] Life is a lot of hassle—so what?!
　　　Pause.
This city was a lot different. Used to be something different—let me tell you—[*beat*] "Zapateria de Discuento," huh?! [*in disgust*] Christ. [*pause*] Low brows—that's who comes to this country, that's who we get, a lot of low brows—[*pause*] We get foreigners—we don't get good ones—we get low brows. That's who comes here, that's all, low brows.
　　　Pause.
I was born in Albany—New York—but Pop moved us out here when I was twelve.
　　　Pause.
[*drawing on cigarette*] If you come here you ought to speak English—learn to speak our language.
PAIGE: I guess.
IKE: Walk down the street here, sounds like the UN [*pause*] What? You're one of those young people— You don't know yet, but one day you'll remember what I'm telling you.
PAIGE: [*shrugs, beat*] Ike, how long you been at this job?
IKE: The shoe store? Oh… Year, year and a half. Perez had just opened it. I'm not really worth a shit as a salesman, that's the funny thing.
PAIGE: [*smiles*] Yeah.
IKE: I've done a lot of it, though.
PAIGE: Being a salesman?
IKE: Sales, uh huh. [*pause*] I'm not ruthless—you gotta be ruthless to be a top salesman. [*pause*] I'm too nice a guy—[*laughs*] That's the problem, you can't be a good guy and still be a top salesman.

Pause.

I got a shoe store joke—Paige?!

PAIGE: Yeah—OK, let's have it.

IKE: There's this woman—her husband's away a lot—a truck driver, and she's gettin' lonely—bored—whatever—so she decides to get a new pair of shoes—cheer herself up. On the way to the shoe store, she realizes she forgot to wear any panties—but, hey, she's almost there... So she's at the store and the salesman is fitting her for a pair of pumps and he glances up—and shit—you know—he can see it all—so he puts down the shoes and says, "Lady—I'd like to have your pussy full of ice cream and then eat it all"—Well—she's shocked and gets up and storms out—and when her husband gets home she says, "Honey—I want you to take care of this salesman at the shoe store" and she tells him the story—and her husband says, "Hold on—hold on, first: you had no business buying another pair of shoes—and second: you had no business leaving home without any panties, and third—I don't fuck with any man can eat that much ice cream."

IKE *bursts into convulsive laughter.*

PAIGE: [*deadpan*] Funny, Ike.

IKE: [*still laughing*] Shoe store joke...right...not a lot of shoe store jokes.

PAIGE: [*not laughing*] Uh huh.

IKE: [*still chuckling*] Damn... [*pause, trying to stop laughing*] ...Well, OK...

IKE, *still chuckling, rubs his wrist and arm.*

PAIGE: Hurt your arm?

IKE: Huh...? I got an infection, I'm taking antibiotics.

> PAIGE *nods. Silence—*IKE *pushes up sleeve.*

See? This red streak here...

> *He indicates lower arm, then tenderly probes the area with finger*

It's a little sore to touch.

PAIGE: Uh huh.

IKE: I went over to the free clinic, they gave me the antibiotics.

PAIGE: It's infected—is it infected?

IKE: It's a staff infection—or a strep infection—I don't know.

PAIGE: And they gave you antibiotics?

IKE: The clinic did—you know, they gave me a few days' worth.

PAIGE: For the infection?

IKE: For the infection, yes.

> PAIGE *nods. Pause. Knock at door.*

PAIGE: [*calls toward door*] Yeah?

> JUNIOR'S *voice outside.*

JUNIOR: It's Junior.

PAIGE: Come on in.

> JUNIOR *enters. He looks a little flushed, maybe a little agitated.*

IKE: Hello, Junior.

JUNIOR: [*nods to* IKE] Ike—Hi, Paige.

> JUNIOR *walks over to the window, then back across the room...*

PAIGE: [*to* JUNIOR] You just get home?

JUNIOR: What? Well—yeah—I just came from the store.

> JUNIOR *sits.*

PAIGE: [*to* JUNIOR] You look tired, man.

JUNIOR: I'm a little tired, yeah—I guess I'm a little tired.
    Pause.
    I gotta work. I gotta go back at seven and help do inventory. [*beat*] My nephew Jack is in town—he's gonna help, too. [*beat*] You know Jack?
    Pause.
    No? No, well, yeah, Jack's my nephew, you know.
    Beat.
    I ever tell you about Jack? [*beat*] My family's got an attitude about Jack. Jack isn't a big topic at, like, the dinner table, you know.
PAIGE: Yeah!?
JUNIOR: My uncle has him coming over for inventory—my uncle doesn't give a shit, you know.
    PAIGE *nods. Pause.*
    Jack's been in trouble. Lots of trouble.
IKE: What kind of trouble?
JUNIOR: [*pause*] I've done worse—you believe it?
IKE: What?
JUNIOR: [*turning away, in disgust*] Shit… [*beat*] I done things before, I mean, people do things, right?! Situations?! You can get in situations—that can't be helped.
IKE: Sure, it happens.
JUNIOR: Sure—the wrong situation, wrong kind of people. [*pause*] But I'm not like Jack—I don't do the shit Jack does.
    IKE *nods, understanding.*
    Sure. You can't dwell on this stuff. I mean I've been in these situations. [*barks a laugh*] Shit. [*beat*] You want me to tell you something?! Huh!?
IKE: I don't know—You want to tell me?

JUNIOR: I've killed a man. [*beat*] I've killed a man before.

> PAIGE *and* IKE *exchange looks. Pause.* JUNIOR
> *lights a cigarette.*

PAIGE: [*with vague edge of irony*] Who'd you kill?

JUNIOR: [*with edge of hostility*] Huh? You want to know
who I killed. Paige?

PAIGE: [*pause*] Yeah, I guess.

> JUNIOR *laughs, shakes head.*

JUNIOR: Shit... Shit. [*chuckles*] Lookit...

> JUNIOR *stands...*

I didn't kill nobody. [*laughs*] I mean, it wouldn't be
real smart to talk about it anyway.

PAIGE: I guess not.

> JUNIOR *keeps pacing.*

JUNIOR: I mean, we don't all know each other that well,
not really.

PAIGE: No.

JUNIOR: We're just neighbors—and we work in the same
shopping center—that don't mean much.

PAIGE: Nope.

> *Pause.*

IKE: Well, I may just hook it up here, go get some food.

JUNIOR: Yeah—I gotta get back to the store.

> JUNIOR *and* IKE *look at each other—Silence.*

Go see my nephew Jack.

IKE: [*thrown away as he stands*] Gotta do what you gotta
do—

JUNIOR: Yeah—my uncle won't discuss Jack—won't talk
about Jack's "problems."

IKE: Might be a smart idea.

JUNIOR: [*getting a little pissed off*] Shit... Jack—fuck Jack
and his piss-ant problems. [*beat*] I got a half-brother,
too—got arrested when he was sixteen for stealing a
car.

>   JUNIOR *has moved over close to* IKE *so they're*
>   *standing face to face.*

What do you think of that? Ike?

IKE: I don't know.

JUNIOR: No? [*beat*] No opinion on that, huh?!

IKE: My arm's startin' to hurt.

JUNIOR: Huh?

>   JUNIOR *backs off.*

IKE: My arm.

>   IKE *holds out arm, pulling sleeve up...*

See?

JUNIOR: What...?

>   JUNIOR *looks at arm tentatively...*

IKE: It's infected.

JUNIOR: Infected?

IKE: Yes.

>   IKE *pulls arm back. Silence.* JUNIOR *walks away.*
>   PAIGE *and* IKE *watch him.*

JUNIOR: You know—Jack tried suicide a few times—more
than once, and he tried with purpose—he was serious. [*pause*] I could tell you about it, I could tell you
all about it.

>   JUNIOR *looks at* IKE *and* PAIGE. *Pause.*

They were always givin' him Stelazine, but well, he'd
always stop takin' it. [*pause*] After a point, he'd always stop takin' it, stop takin' his medication. [*pause*]
He'd have his relapses, see, then, he'd have one of

his episodes. But he'd leave AMA—leave—AMAed himself—Against Medical Advice—Leave against the
doctor's advice, OK?!

Silence.

[*quieter*] It's a damn shame. A damn shame. I gotta
lot of feelings for Jack, you know. I mean, Jack's family—right?! You don't just blow off your family. You
got to take care of family—protect family—you can't
just leave 'em out there—leave 'em hanging—that
woudn't be right, would it? [*beat*] That wouldn't be
right at all. It's not somethin' I'd feel good about. Not
something I'd want to live with. I mean, whatever I
think of Jack, whatever I think of Jack's problems—
I'm not gonna just abandon him, I'm not that kind of
person, I just wasn't brought up that way—

Lights fade out.

Lights up: IKE *seated, blanket over shoulders.* PAIGE
seated nearby. It's quiet outside. Both are smoking.
Silence.

IKE: A scientist. My father would say that was the high-
est type of intelligence. [*pause*] I figured, so, I'd be a
scientist. Some kind of scientist. I think he never
thought that was what I'd be. He wasn't expecting
me to amount to much. [*pause*] I ended up sellin'
cars. When I got out of high school I stumbled into
this job sellin' Fords. I actually was mostly selling
Ford trucks. There is no little call for trucks in Albany. At least then—this is some time ago. Then I
met this fella, came in to buy a truck—and we took
this test drive, and he was talkin' about his work—

and it sounded a lot better than sellin' Ford trucks, and he liked me, and he wasn't much older than me really. He was able to travel a good deal, and I liked that—I was thinkin' that maybe leaving Albany would be a good idea. I just did it—this young man's name was Raymond—and I just quit my job and I never told my mom or dad—I phoned them later—and I explained what I'd done. My father just sort of said something—mumbled—he was gruff—and then gave the phone to my mom. [*long pause*] I didn't see him again for twelve years.

    Pause.

PAIGE: What was the job? What did this Raymond do?

IKE: He worked for a chain of motels—which was still a kind of fresh idea—motels—[*beat*] He went from one to another, checking on them. So I started doing the same thing, he sort of trained me. His father practically owned the company. [*laughs*]

    Silence.

You had a little check list—how was the bed made, things like that.

PAIGE: Where'd you go after that?

IKE: I'm not sure. [*pause*] I was hurt, this time, down south, at an amusement park. I worked the tram, and we crashed—and my head went through the windshield. This scar here—[*indicates scar*] There, it looked much worse then. The boy driving, he knew it was his fault and for goddamn months he'd apologize to me. I finally told him to stop. The scar wasn't bad—you can see that, it's just a little bitty line here. [*pause*] Funny little guy that tram driver. [*pause*] Eventually

guys like me end up in sales—all kinds of things—
Christ—I've sold a lot of stuff. I worked for Forest Lawn
when I first came out here. I came out with this girl,
and she'd won a beauty contest and got a free trip
out to Hollywood so I came out with her. We cashed
in her plane ticket, and drove out. Straight from Chicago. It was winter and I remember how good it felt
to leave Chicago.

PAIGE: What was her name?

IKE: [*thinking for a moment*] Dorothy. [*pause*] I had always wanted a girl like Dorothy, you know, a beauty
queen type of girl. [*pause*] Anyway, I sold plots at
Forest Lawn that year. I worked under a Mister
Adamis—a little man who'd been there a long time, a
long time.

PAIGE: You ever get married?

IKE: No, uh, uh, never did. Never had any children,
either.

PAIGE: What about Dorothy?

IKE: [*shrugs*] She went back home. She didn't get any
movie parts, so I guess she figured, I don't know, she'd
go back, to be close to her mom.

    Pause.

PAIGE: I was married,—well, I'm still married.

    IKE *nods. Pause.*

To this black guy, Deak. [*pause*] I never see him now.
[*pause*] He wasn't much—he wasn't good to me.
[*pause*] I was twenty-one, had just turned twenty-
one. Fuck—he was about thirty, and he hadn't much
luck, and I think, you know, I wanted him to have a
few good breaks—[*laughs dryly*] But I was just another bad break, as it turned out.

IKE: [*pause*] What did your parents think?

PAIGE: About Deak? Shit—they wouldn't talk to me. Barely talk to me now.

> IKE *is shivering a bit more...*

How you doin', Ike? How you feel?

IKE: My arm hurts.

PAIGE: You're sweating.

IKE: The antibiotics should help. They'll start having effect soon.

> PAIGE *nodding. Pause.*

PAIGE: How do you get a staff infection?

IKE: [*smiles*] You just get 'em—like invisible forces, floating around and they attach themselves to you— they just move through you, into you somehow... [*smiles*]

> IKE *pulls blanket closer around himself. Silence.*

PAIGE: Deak used to drink that wine, you know—get himself that fortified shit. He got sick, he got pneumonia—walking pneumonia. And he didn't take care of it and so it got worse and he ended up in the hospital.

IKE: I don't drink anymore—I used to, but, I just don't anymore.

> *Silence.*

PAIGE: I drank when I was with Deak. If he drank, I drank. That's what I did with him, it's about all I did with him.

> *Silence.*

IKE: I don't ever get out of the city anymore—I hardly ever get to go anywhere. [*pause*] Last time I went anywhere—I went to Santa Anita. Used to take the bus, catch it up at the Biltmore—about an hour's ride.

Last time I did this was July—How many months is that?

PAIGE: Six.

IKE: Yeah. [*pause*] Used to go with this guy Emory—a little Armenian guy, real into health food, worked as a salesman, too—I worked with him, under him, worked sunglasses. [*pause*] He gave me the northern route through San Luis Obispo—selling "Sun-smile" sunglasses, mostly to drug stores. I'd hit towns like Castroville, you see, where there were maybe two drug stores—actually Castroville had only one for awhile I think—a Rexall—and I'd set the place with a line of glasses, different styles, and we had quality stuff, with like a floor rack next to the suntan lotion, and a counter display by the pharmacist. Emory had other things, too—this was seventy-one—so we had stuff like those little string mandalas—you know, that you made yourself, and posters, and for a while these small candles in different shapes, different styles—one was a little guy and his dog...

PAIGE: The candles?

IKE: What?

PAIGE: I don't understand.

IKE: The candles were actually shaped into little figures and the biggest seller, by far, the biggest seller was the "Nose-Picker"—[*laughs*] A little Jewish-looking guy with his finger stuck up his nose—we sold out of that one before Thanksgiving one year. [*pause*] Emory sold his interest in the company to his brother—that's when I quit—I didn't get along with his brother. You don't meet many nice people in that kind of job—

but, well, pharmacists weren't really businessmen, most of them,...

    IKE *gets up during this to pace—emphasizing certain points.*

...and they were very distrustful, mostly, and they just acted like you were trying to take advantage of them—right off, they just were on the defensive, and they'd question everything, and bitch at you over stuff that, things, stuff that had no importance—matters that they didn't know anything about—these guys didn't know anything about sunglasses and you'd have to argue about where to put the racks, that kind of thing, and... it was just hard, you know, drive all day up to some run down old Rexall in Fresno, try to come on all sunny and positive... I'd always wear these white shoes and checked pants, a very "up" image, which is important—and I had a bright yellow laminated card with an orange sun wearing sunglasses—and my name—it was a total package—no question about it.

    IKE *has run out of energy. He sits.* PAIGE *gets up and helps put blanket over shoulders.*

PAIGE: You want some tea—I'll put some lemon in it?

IKE: Huh? [*pauses, breathing hard*] ...Oh, no, no thanks.

PAIGE: Maybe we should take you over to the emergency room?

IKE: [*shakes head "no"*] I'm all right—I got these things...

    IKE *holds up bottle of antibiotics...*

I can't read this—well...

    Puts them back in pocket.

PAIGE: I was gonna go get some Chinese take out—or

Thai—whatever that place over there is. [*pause*] You want some soup?

IKE: Paige?

> *Pause—*PAIGE *waiting. Silence.*

PAIGE: What?

IKE: [*pause*] I was never close to my father, never intimate. I never got close to him.

> IKE *looks up at her.*
> *Lights fade out.*

> *Lights up slowly:* JUNIOR *standing alone in room. He mumbles something to himself, we can't hear what, and punches open hand with his fist. He turns, swearing to himself, his body tense. He takes several steps, stops, turns back, says something more that we are unable to hear. In shadows we now see* PAIGE, *watching.* JUNIOR *points his finger at invisible antagonist.*

JUNIOR: [*to invisible antagonist*] That's what I said—that is what I mean—[*under his breath*] Fuck him.

> *He turns away. He goes and sits. Silence.* PAIGE *advances slowly.* JUNIOR *turns to look at her. Silence, they stare at each other a long time.*

[*quietly, evenly*] I feel powerful.

> PAIGE *nods. Silence.*

Paige?

> PAIGE *waits...*

There is nothing more I can do to help myself. [*pause*] There is nothing more I can do to help myself. [*long pause*] We could go someplace?!

PAIGE: Maybe.

JUNIOR: I can't let it get me down.

PAIGE: No.

> *Pause.* PAIGE *steps behind* JUNIOR.

JUNIOR: [*not looking at* PAIGE] They make demands on me.

> PAIGE *nods and gently runs her fingers over his ears and hair. She touches him on neck tenderly. Silence.*

Families are like that, they demand—and today I got a parking ticket...a forty dollar parking ticket.

> *He turns and looks up at* PAIGE.

[*pause*] I don't want to give them forty dollars—I don't make enough. You see?! That's not fair.

PAIGE: [*quietly*] Just pay it.

> *Silence.*

JUNIOR: I cried when I got home—when I got the ticket. [*beat*] I put it down on the table—it's pink, and the guy had circled "forty dollars"—and I went to the kitchen and when I got to the kitchen I started to cry. That's really shitty—my getting that ticket.

> *Silence.* PAIGE *walks off a few steps, lights cigarette.*

PAIGE: I was thinking about Deak.

JUNIOR: Uh huh.

PAIGE: Nothing, that's all.

JUNIOR: You thought about Deak. Fuck him. Paige? Fuck him, OK?!

PAIGE: I gotta pick up Ike. [*pause*] He should be outta there by now.

JUNIOR: [*starting to get up*] No—Look—emergency rooms take forever.

JUNIOR *stops...*

PAIGE: [*beat*] I called—they said he'd be done by now.
They look at each other. Pause.

I don't want him to be waiting there. [*pause*] Junior?
Junior, Ike's sick—he's gotta rest.

JUNIOR: Yeah—of course.

Pause.

[*nodding*] Rest is what you gotta do with infection.

PAIGE: [*pause*] Let's go get him, come on.

JUNIOR *stands...*

[*pause*] Ike's not gonna be able to work.

JUNIOR: Yeah...well.. [*shrugs*]

PAIGE: Junior, let's go now...

JUNIOR: [*pause*] Deak... I met Deak once, remember?

PAIGE: Yeah.

JUNIOR: The skinny black guy, right?

PAIGE: Yeah.

JUNIOR: I didn't like him.

PAIGE: Not many people did.

JUNIOR: He was a "marginal" person.

PAIGE: I don't think we should talk about Deak.

JUNIOR: I didn't like how he complained all the time.

PAIGE: Deak doesn't matter now.

JUNIOR: I don't want to listen to that complaining shit.
I don't want to listen to it, simple as that.

PAIGE: You don't have to.

JUNIOR *looks at her. Pause.*

[*quietly*] I want you to feel better.

JUNIOR: [*pause*] I don't have to put up with that from
anyone—don't you see that—

PAIGE: I see.

JUNIOR: You put up with it—it can make you anxious.

PAIGE: Deak used to say, "Bite the scorpion," you know—
if you're gonna get down—you "bite the scorpion"—
you don't just talk—talk is cheap. Conversation, there
is nothing cheaper than conversation.

    Pause. PAIGE *looks at him, then turns away.*

I just want to pay the rent. Simple things. I'd like to
just know the rent will be there. [*pause*] If you work,
that things will get better. That's all, that's all. [*pause*]
You ever drive through Beverly Hills, Brentwood, and
wonder where did all these people get money—how
did they all get so much money. There's a *lot* of nice
houses we're talking about. A lot.

JUNIOR: You don't live there. You don't exist in that
part of the world. It's different there.

PAIGE: [*pause*] Yes, it is all different. [*pause*] I'd like not
to have to drive through those areas.

JUNIOR: The rich—being near the rich, there's this stuff,
invisible, and it attaches itself to you and you carry
it around on you.

    JUNIOR *steps over to her.*

When I'm around the rich I have to go home and
wash—wash that stuff off. It gets all over you—and
you can't let it stay on you—because it's toxic—it's
poison shit.

    Pause.

PAIGE: I'm gonna stop going through those places.

    JUNIOR *steps closer still.*

You gotta "bite the scorpion," Junior—

    JUNIOR *nods.*

You gotta do it now.

JUNIOR: I don't have to hide anymore.

PAIGE: No.

> JUNIOR *puts open palm of his hand on her face. Silence. He takes it away.*

JUNIOR:—People can get to you if you let them. [*pause*] You know my favorite song—? It's "Angel of Love"...It's from the fifties, my older brother—my step brother... He had a lot of old 45s and "Angel of Love" was my favorite.

> JUNIOR *leans closer...*

I didn't ever kill anyone. [*pause*] Jack did I think, but I can't be sure. [*pause*] If I'd ever killed anyone it would have been Deak. [*pause*] I don't like to think about killing—it's a horrible thing, killing, murder.

> PAIGE *reaches out and touches his lips, then pulls her fingers back.* JUNIOR *looks down at her skirt.*

I like when you wear tight skirts.

PAIGE: Yeah? Good.

JUNIOR: The world is full of bad things, bad people. I don't think I'm a bad person. Do you?

PAIGE: No.

> JUNIOR *is rubbing his body up against her.*

JUNIOR: I never killed anyone.

> *Pause. They rub against each other without using hands.*

I like tight skirts.

> *Pause.* PAIGE *licks his neck...* PAIGE *sinks slowly to her knees.*

PAIGE: I don't think you're a bad person.

> *She unzips his fly slowly.*

JUNIOR: Are you going to kiss me.

PAIGE *nods...*
Are we going to kiss all the way.

At this point a spot starts coming up very slowly on IKE, *stage right, on bus bench. Light doesn't come up full on* IKE *until end.* IKE *looks tired, sick. At some point he lights a cigarette.*

PAIGE *slips her hand inside his fly, stroking him...*
[*tense*] Kiss me all the way... [*pause*] Paige, kiss me all the way.

She keeps stroking, JUNIOR *becoming ever more aroused.*

PAIGE: I will, I'm going to.

JUNIOR: I'm clean. Paige. [*beat*] I don't have to take shit from people anymore. You know that don't you.

PAIGE *nods. He takes her head in his hands— they stare at each other.*

PAIGE: The world is full of terrible things, I know it is.

JUNIOR: I'm a clean and good person. [*pause*] I am clean.

PAIGE: Yes.

JUNIOR *lets go of her head. She starts to put her mouth on him.*

JUNIOR: I'm so scared.

Lights fading out on them—up full now on IKE.
Lights are out on JUNIOR *and* PAIGE.
Holds on IKE*—lights out.*

END

SEA OF CORTEZ

Sea of Cortez, directed by the author and David Schweizer, was first presented at the Cast Theatre in Hollywood on April 24, 1992, with the following cast:

MANCE	John Horn
EDDIE	George Gerdes
FORTUNE TELLER	Lee Kissman
TRANSLATOR	Soumaya Aakaboune
MALONE	John C. McLaughlin
DR COUSA	Harvey Perr
DR FRENCH	Mick Collins
RUSS	Ron Campbell

ACT 1

Pin spot up slowly on a man standing on platform—upstage center. All we see are his legs from knee down. He's wearing neatly pressed pinstripe trousers and a pair of highly polished cordovan wing tip shoes.

VOICE [*Offstage*, MANCE]: It was raining, very heavily. This rain went on all night, continuously, the entire night, without any let up. The men would come to the door, and they'd knock. It was a loosely fitted door—and it sounded loud. The men would be let in—and I could see them, I could see their feet and they all wore boots, and their boots were muddy—and the floor got dirtier and more full of mud as the night wore on. My head rested on the floor, the side of my head against the floor and the blood ran from my head toward the door. The blood looked almost black. There wasn't much light inside the house. The boots made a lot of noise on the wood floor, and with my ear and head against the hardwood I also felt the vibration of their steps. I don't remember what anyone said—or if they ever spoke at all. I think maybe nobody spoke. I could hear a car engine outside now and again—and I could hear the rain. [*pause*] I always wore good shoes, English shoes, and I kept them clean and polished. I liked my trousers cuffed, and I pre-

127

ferred a single break. I always dressed well, and I kept myself clean, even out there. [*pause*]. All I could see, as I lay there, was their legs and boots, the mud caking on their heels and soles, and the shadows, and my blood spreading across the planks of the floor. I fell unconscious at some point but when I woke nothing was any different. I heard a dog barking, out in the yard, to the side, probably chained to a tree or to a stake.

> *Pin spot slowly fades out.*
>
> *Lights up slowly. An old man,* FORTUNE TELLER, *sits with young girl,* TRANSLATOR, *behind small table and in front of canvas hanging with esoteric scribbling, graphs, drawings of palms—feet—eyes—etc.* EDDIE *enters—sits at table.*

FORTUNE TELLER: [*fast—emphatic—stuttering*] Ah,ah, ah, ah, ah, ah, ah, ah, ah, uh,uh,uh... ah, ah, ah, ah, ah, ah, ah, ah, ah...

> *Slapping* EDDIE'S *palm.*

Ah, ah, ah, ah, ah, ah, ah, ah, eh, eh, eh, eh, cha, cha, cha, cha, cha, cha, cha, cha, cha, cha, cha, ...ah, ah, ah, ah...

> *Pointing to palm as he looks at* WOMAN TRANSLATOR.

Eeh, eeh, eeh, eeh, eeh, eeh...

> *He pauses to study palm, looking at it closely with his crossed eyes.*

Mmmm... mmm,... ah, ah, ah...

> *He slaps palm again, then turns it over—using magnifying glass to examine the small lines on edge of hand.*

Oh, oh, oh, oh, oh... ch, ch, ch, ch, ch, ch, ch, ch, ch, ch, ch, ch, ch, ch, ch, ch...

> *He nodding rapidly now, turning hand over and over, looking at both sides...*

TRANSLATOR: [*with heavy accent*] Your name?...he asks your name.

EDDIE: [*beat*] Eddie.

> *She looks over at* FORTUNE TELLER, *then back to* EDDIE.

TRANSLATOR: Now you've come here. Eddie?

FORTUNE TELLER: Ch, ch, ch, ch, ch, ch...

> FORTUNE TELLER *pointing out something on* EDDIE'S *palm to* TRANSLATOR.

TRANSLATOR: Without your wife?

EDDIE: I have no wife.

FORTUNE TELLER: [*tapping* EDDIE'S *palm*] Ch, ch, ch, ch, ch, ch, ch, ch, ch, ch, ch, ch, ch, ch, ch, ch, ch...

> TRANSLATOR *listening intently to* FORTUNE TELLER.

Ch, ah, ah, ah, ah, ah, ah, ah, ah, ah, ah...

EDDIE: What's he saying?

TRANSLATOR: He says the night is warm–[*pause*] Are you afraid?

EDDIE: [*pause*] No, uh uh–

TRANSLATOR: You are alone?

EDDIE: [*beats*] I don't know.

> *Silence.*

TRANSLATOR: You want to give gold to the saints?

EDDIE: Excuse me?

TRANSLATOR: For saints.

FORTUNE TELLER *holds up strip of gold leaf...*
EDDIE: How much?

TRANSLATOR *looks confused.*

How much?

TRANSLATOR *looks to* FORTUNE TELLER.
FORTUNE TELLER: Ah, ah, ah, ah, ah,

FORTUNE TELLER *slaps gold leaf in* EDDIE'S *palm, then turns to* TRANSLATOR. *She looks to* EDDIE.
TRANSLATOR: For the saints—

EDDIE *smiles, takes money from pocket. He gives it to* FORTUNE TELLER *who then smooths gold leaf out on* EDDIE'S *palm. She closes* EDDIE'S *hand into fist and blows on it—then slaps it on all sides, and slowly opens it... the gold leaf is gone.*

Gone.

EDDIE: Yeah.

TRANSLATOR: To the saints.

FORTUNE TELLER *leans back, smiles.*

Much luck—for you. Much good luck.

EDDIE *nods slowly.*
Lights fade out.

Lights up: veranda of clinic. MALONE *stands to side,* DR COUSA *paces downstage.* EDDIE *sits.*
DR COUSA: No, no, ...OK...

He looks back—at EDDIE.

Are we referring to, what? The AMA? Excuse me... ah... the "American" medical mafia—ah, is that... the "American" medical dictatorship—OK?! All right—yes— the AMA [*beats*] Right. Absolutely, absolutely. Just so, just so. [*snorts a derisive laugh*] The *American* Medical Association. Are we in Baja? Are we in Mexico?

    Stops—looks around...

Mexico—Mexico. [*beats*] It's a desert out there. [*beats*] OK. My certificate is from the University of Colorado—it hangs "On-the-Wall"—in my office. [*beat*] Let's see—let us look at what kind of energy exists in the body.

    He advances on MALONE.

Are your eyes clear? Alert? Breath clean and free moving? Can I ask of your blood? Let me ask you—what do you eat? I was born in Brooklyn—I grew up there, in the grime, in the noise—eating grease and fats—oils, fats, sugar [*beat*] Brooklyn, New York—and I could see my father die of heart disease, and my mother die of complications from alcoholism—with gout, glaucoma, she wore thick ugly lenses on her glasses—and her arms were bruised from the slightest touch and she'd grown fat and grotesque—my mother—once a beauty queen, grown nearly monstrous—[*beats*] this amazing organism—the body—the human corporeal body—but without the spirit you will reach only partial conclusions—only part, a part—of—the—story. Huh?! OK—only a part! Only, only—a—part! [*beats*] There is such complexity—the human body. Our body must be respected, respected, and feared! [*beats*] I fear the body,—give it nothing to use against you—it will punish without hesitation—it will condemn all of us eventually.

    DR COUSA *stares at* EDDIE—*then steps toward him.*

I am in Mexico so I can do the work I believe in. I do not make a great deal of money. [*pause*] You do not know the treatment here. Russ—perhaps you will meet Russ—Russ was originally diagnosed with Schwannoma of the left cerebella—pontine angle.

DR COUSA *gently pokes his fingers against* EDDIE's *head.*

The usual operation is through a small opening in the posterior occipital region. Here.

DOC COUSA *pokes* EDDIE's *head again.*

Russ had lost use of his tongue—his fingers had lost most of their feeling and even his vision had become impaired. His doctor—in Virginia—told him at best he would never walk—or speak correctly, and probably would not live more than two years. [*beats*] When I first saw Russ he could barely find his way into the room. His equilibrium was worsening. His legs were becoming spastic. The corner of the mouth deviated to the left. It was a tragic sight. [*pause*] That was four and a half years ago. [*beats*] We do not drill holes in anyone's head. [*pause*] There are no miracles.There is only, simply put, "common sense." Nature provides— the orchards, the fields, the forests—there is abundance here on earth. We only have to resist giving in to the wretchedness of modern life—see?!—I tell you this with great humility. I cannot cure—none of us can. I can only point you toward what nature has always offered to us. See?!

DR COUSA *now pacing between* MALONE *and* EDDIE.

OK... OK... these are disturbing times—distressing times, and we have plagues, we have madness— people abusing their own children. Huh!? I am driven from my own country. Driven to foreign shores to practice what I believe to be sincere and honest treatment. And let me tell you—you are free to go anywhere, look at anything—the clinic is open to visitors—I only ask that you let us know, let one of the attendants know that you are here. I want to share, I do not do this for profit. [*pause*] Let me tell you both, this is a place of goodness, or so I believe. Let me tell you both—this is my sincere belief—sincere—I tell you this, as I always do—this is a place of goodness.

    Silence.

    Lights fade out.

    Lights fade up slowly: MANCE'S *room. Seated in wheelchair is* MANCE—*he looks frail, wears tinted glasses and has a shawl on his lap. Seated to side is* EDDIE.

MANCE: Almonds... almonds.

    He looks at EDDIE. *Pause.*

Raw—you must eat them raw. [*beat*] Eddie?

EDDIE: Yeah.

MANCE: Eddie... [*pauses, thinking*] there's a warmth here—comes up from the ground.

    MANCE *stares at* EDDIE. *Silence.*

EDDIE: Can I get you anything?

    MANCE *pulls the shawl tighter around his legs.*

MANCE: In my next life—maybe I'll come back as one of the scorpions here. [*pause*]... in my next life. [*beat*] An Emperor scorpion.

    Silence. MANCE *slowly wheels himself over toward terrace...*

The prostitutes down in town—they have girls, four-teen, fifteen—very young girls—in China, the rich Chinese—rich Chinese gentlemen, believe that if they sleep with young girls—that sleeping with ten or eleven year old girls will prolong their life. Increase longevity [*smiles, pause*]... the Chinese prize longevity—they revere the man who attains great age.

EDDIE *stands, looking out through curtains.*

EDDIE: I think it's a little overrated. [*beat*] Long life.

EDDIE *turns and looks at* MANCE—*pause.*

MANCE: Long life.

EDDIE: You think it's OK to drink the soda pop here?

MANCE: I believe it is.

EDDIE: I wasn't sure, you know—with this whole deal about the water. [*pause*] I could really use a Coke. [*pause*] What about the ice cubes? In restaurants—say, when the ice cubes melt...? What about that?

MANCE: I don't think you should worry.

They continue to stare at each other. Pause.

EDDIE: [*cold, with edge*] Well—good—that's a relief.

Silence. EDDIE *walks around* MANCE.

I've never been out of the country, never been to Mexico. [*beats*] This is my first time. First time out of the United States.

MANCE: Travel broadens one's perspective.

EDDIE *pauses, leans in...*

EDDIE: You don't look the same, last time I saw you.

MANCE *looks at him. Silence.*

Malone came with me. [*pause*] He isn't one for traveling much either. [*beats*] He feels like I do—doesn't see the allure.

EDDIE *paces–going back over to veranda. Silence.*

Makes you appreciate the United States.

MANCE: Where's Malone?

EDDIE: We got a room,–a little hotel–twenty bucks a night. Air conditioned.

EDDIE *turns back–looking at* MANCE.

Malone came today–but he left. Said he'd come by tomorrow.

MANCE: I see.

EDDIE: I think he was gonna do some fishing.

MANCE *nods very slowly. Pause.*

One of those half day boats. [*pause*] Sea of Cortez– what they call it, right?!

MANCE: [*nods*] Sea of Cortez.

Pause. Lights fade down until only wheelchair is lit. EDDIE *steps over to* MANCE *in wheelchair. He stands behind chair...*

EDDIE: You in a lot of pain, Mance?

MANCE *says nothing.*

It's something, you know–it's big–it's a very big thing, what happens to your body.

MANCE *sits silently. Pause.* EDDIE *steps away from chair.*

Wouldn't you agree? Like one's lost–lost in the wilderness–stumbling along and falling... [*beats*] [*leans in close to* MANCE] The fuck do you do? You've become your own enemy–it's a lot to try and think about.

EDDIE *straightens up...*

[*pause*] They let me in–you know–even though it's

too early for visitors. They saw my name, when I signed in, saw it was McTier too. Didn't know I was just your stepson—I didn't tell 'em that. Saw no need to.
Silence.
Seldom seen and hard to find. [*pause*] That's how I like to do it. [*beats*] Seldom seen and hard to find.
Lights fading slowly out as EDDIE *backs away.*

Lights up slowly: Veranda of clinic. DR FRENCH *stands to side. He has on lab coat, white pants and white bucks.* RUSS *stands in pajamas, he's dirty, barefoot, out of breath.*

DR FRENCH: [*gently*] What was it like?
No answer.

Russ? [*pause*] What was it like? In your own words—
RUSS *looks at him, still out of breath...*

Let's get you a glass of juice. [*beats*] Orange juice.

RUSS: [*hesitant–scared*] Do you think... my feet... have I permanently damaged my feet... you think I might have—Doctor?

DR FRENCH *strolls closer—still very gently, exceedingly calm...*

DR FRENCH: Russ?

RUSS: Doctor?

DR FRENCH: It was dark on the beach.

RUSS: And there were rocks—

DR FRENCH: I know it must have been very dark.
RUSS *stares at him. Pause.*

Dark and rocky. A quarter moon over the water—and everything was quiet.

RUSS *nods.*

RUSS: [*softly*] There was only the sound of the waves.

    DR FRENCH *nods...*

DR FRENCH: Russ?

RUSS: Yes?

DR FRENCH: [*beats*] Let's sit together.

    RUSS *nods as* DR FRENCH *pulls up two chairs.*
    They sit. Pause. DR FRENCH *pats* RUSS *on the thigh.*
I want to hear about it in your own words. [*pause*]
Do you want that orange juice now?

RUSS: [*beats*] Perhaps a blanket?

    DR FRENCH *stands slowly.*

DR FRENCH: Russ... I will accompany you—until I can
no longer be of use.

RUSS: I was quite active at one time.

DR FRENCH: That was another time.

RUSS: Yes.

DR FRENCH: [*pause*] We both understand that something about our old "Russ," there was something that
allowed the tumors to advance in the way they did...
something that maybe, even "crafted" them.

    RUSS *nods.*

You cannot let yourself lose control, Russ.

RUSS: I feel on the other side of this wall... When I'm
out there... I... it can seem... at times, at moments,
that I am some part of a herd—a lost herd of exotic
animals. [*beats*] Roaming around, just as we please.

DR FRENCH: We've talked about our dreams, about
the emotions.

RUSS: The clouds at night—casting outlines...that our

herd recognizes. It's part of our nervous system, these outlines.

DR FRENCH *looks at him a moment, then places a hand on his shoulder...*

DR FRENCH: Who does the tumor belong to?

RUSS: It belongs to me. To Russ.

DR FRENCH *squeezes his shoulder.*

DR FRENCH: It belongs to you. It belongs to Russ.

RUSS *nods slowly as the lights fade out.*
Light and sound black out.

Lights up slowly—twilight, beach, Sea of Cortez.
MALONE *and* EDDIE.

MALONE: She knew Mance.

EDDIE: I saw her. Did you know that?

MALONE: When? When'd you see her? [*beats*] She looked bad there at the end.

EDDIE: Mance would send her money. He never gave that much.

MALONE: Back when I met her—she would model at trade shows. She would stand in the back of a pick-up—wearing a bikini—eight, nine hours a day—in places like San Bernadino, Tucson, wherever. I met her she was doing an auto parts show in Las Vegas. Three days we had a room at the Tropicana. You talk about fun—we had some. She was just twenty-four then—with the whitest skin I ever saw.

EDDIE: She went blind you know?!

MALONE: I knew that, yeah.

Silence. MALONE *paces down by the water.*

EDDIE: I'd only see Mance—oh—twice, three times a year.

MALONE: Uh huh.

EDDIE: [*pause*] It may be hard—you know—to get back…after dark, to get back, in the dark. [*beats*] Malone?

MALONE: She met me once, out at Joshua Tree—at twilight. I stood by my car waiting, as it got dark all around, and you'd start to hear noises in the rocks, in the Cholla cactus, in the Yucca… and every set of headlights that came past I'd think were hers… and then just as complete darkness took hold she came—in a little car—I don't know—a small compact car—and she pulled up, and it was her.

EDDIE: Gonna ruin my shoes—walking back in the dark.
>   *It's completely dark now—the only illumination comes from moonlight. Pause.*

MALONE: The old fucker is gonna die. He's a dead man. [*beat*] Death bed sick and graveyard bound.
>   MALONE *turns back to face* EDDIE.

I don't hate him. I got nothing in particular against Mance. [*pause*] I came here—I wanted to talk to him, that's all. I've known him forty years. [*pause*] Forty, maybe forty-two. Forty-two years—so I wanted us to talk. Nothing else.

EDDIE: He doesn't ever say anything good about you man.

MALONE: No? Well—what difference does that make? [*beat*] You think that makes a difference?

EDDIE: It would to me.

MALONE: [*beat*] Uh huh.

MALONE *slowly turns away—takes a deep breath.*
Now—you can't actually see the water anymore. You can't see it, so it becomes something else.

EDDIE: You're a boring old fuck sometimes—you know it?!

MALONE: I know.

EDDIE: I spoke with him. [*pause*] I've been here a day and a half and my mood keeps getting worse.

MALONE *nods and starts to walk back from the water's edge...*

MALONE: Over forty years. [*beats*] If you saw her at the end—you've got no idea—she wasn't the same person. She'd become so sick.

EDDIE: Uh huh.

MALONE: Eddie... you react—see, and you get fooled. You react to the first thing, the first thing is not the real thing and you let yourself get fooled.

EDDIE: You're about broke—isn't that right?

MALONE: Just about right.

EDDIE: Am I fooled about this too? I don't think so.

MALONE: I don't know.

EDDIE: You're sixty something and broke and talking to me about gettin' fooled?

They look at each other—pause. MALONE *turns away.*

MALONE: It's not easy to die away from home. [*pause*] It's not easy being old—sick—and you gotta come down to this shithole—[*pause*]

He looks back at EDDIE.

Give me a hand Eddie...

EDDIE *starts to offer him a hand as light and sound crossfade and* EDDIE *walks into fortune teller stall...*

Lights coming up on FORTUNE TELLER, *who sits behind the small wood table. The* TRANSLATOR *stands in rear by the hanging canvas diagrams etc.* EDDIE *approaches...*

FORTUNE TELLER: Ah, ah, ah, ah, ah, ah, ah, ah, ah... ah... ah...

FORTUNE TELLER *slapping his own palm.* EDDIE *watches him. The* TRANSLATOR *steps over and sits next to* FORTUNE TELLER. *She whispers in his ear. She nods as she looks over at* EDDIE.

EDDIE: Here.

EDDIE *takes out wallet, opens it, pulling out a couple bills.* FORTUNE TELLER *whispers some more to* TRANSLATOR. EDDIE *stands, offering bills.*

What's the matter?

EDDIE *steps closer, arm still outstretched offering bills.* FORTUNE TELLER *whispers again to* TRANSLATOR. *She then looks up at* EDDIE.

TRANSLATOR: Sit down, here.

She pulls out chair for him. EDDIE *sits, money still in his hand.* FORTUNE TELLER *pulls out paper pad, an old worn leather bound book and magnifying glass...*

Give him your hand.

EDDIE *extends hand without money,* FORTUNE TELLER *takes it—examining it closely under magnifying glass.*

FORTUNE TELLER: Ah, ah, ah, ah, eh, eh, eh, eh...
> FORTUNE TELLER *leans over to look in his book, then returns to* EDDIE'S *hand.*

Ah, ah, ah, eh, ah, eh, ah, eh, eeeh, eeeh, eeeh, eeeh, eeeh, ahh, ahh, ahh...
> FORTUNE TELLER *leans over mumbling—stuttering to* TRANSLATOR. *She nods, then looks at* EDDIE.

TRANSLATOR: Says, you lost your mother—before.. ahm... when you were very small.

EDDIE: My mother only died last year.
> FORTUNE TELLER *whispers to* TRANSLATOR.

TRANSLATOR: You lost her. [*beats*] She was lost to you— [*beat*] You were a young boy.
> FORTUNE TELLER *grabs his hand again, looking at it closely...*

FORTUNE TELLER: K, k, k, k, k, k, k, k, k, k, k, k, k, k, k, k, k, k, k, k, k, k, k, k, k, k, k, k, k, k...

TRANSLATOR: You were not well.

EDDIE: What?

FORTUNE TELLER: Ah, ah, ah, ah.
> FORTUNE TELLER *leans in quickly to whisper something to* TRANSLATOR...

TRANSLATOR: Says a sick little boy—

EDDIE: I was?

TRANSLATOR: Huh? Yes, yes. You.

FORTUNE TELLER: K, k, k, k, k, k, k, k, k, k, k, k, k, k, k, k, k, k, k, k, k, k, k, k, k, k, k...

TRANSLATOR: Says you step out... ah... step away, out from under the wings of death.
> EDDIE *smiles...*

EDDIE: Yeah? OK.

FORTUNE TELLER: Kkkkk…

TRANSLATOR: The wings spread out low…

FORTUNE TELLER: Kkk…

TRANSLATOR: The shadow spreads out over the sea…
Over the sea, and over the land.

You will come back? Please?

Lights out.

Lights up. Veranda.

DR COUSA: Eddie…. Join us. [*beats*] Edward—how are you this day?

EDDIE: Me—I'm fine.

DR COUSA: Have you met my colleague, Dr. French.

DR FRENCH *smiles, extends hand.* EDDIE *and* DR FRENCH *shake.*

Dr. French founded this clinic with me when my original site in Bermuda was closed.

DR COUSA *brings a chair over for* EDDIE, *who sits…*

Here Edward, have a seat. You appear a little tired, a little fatigued. [*to* MANCE] Doesn't he? A little under the weather?

MANCE: Yes. He does. A little.

DR COUSA: We were discussing the Hunza Valley, in Pakistan. Have you heard of the Hunzas?

EDDIE: Afraid not, no.

DR COUSA: Well—in the 1950s it was discovered that there was no cancer of any kind among the peoples of the Hunza Valley.

DOC COUSA *stares intently at* EDDIE.

I traveled to Hunza—I researched this phenomenon myself—personally. I was a young physician then, and had decided to specialize in oncology. I wanted the truth.

DR COUSA *suddenly steps over to* EDDIE—
Did you know there is no cancer in the animal kingdom?

EDDIE: Never thought about it.

DR COUSA: Diet—we poison ourselves from without—and "emotion"—we poison ourselves from within. It all interacts Eddie—and it all happens in multiple stages—there is no single casual agent. There are "initiators" Ed, and they are acted upon—by "promoters"—and then only after a latency period.

DR COUSA *strolls downstage...*
Eddie, do you understand the treatment here?

EDDIE: Do I "understand" it?

DR COUSA: In the late 50s the medical establishment in the United States began to persecute those of us who were trying to find alternative treatments—I even fought fluoridation—which you're too young to remember.

He steps closer to EDDIE *again...*
My father was Egyptian—he left Cairo when I was two years old. Know what Cousa means in Egyptian? [*beat*] Squash, it means squash—the vegetable. [*smiles*] Dr Squash huh? [*laughs*]

EDDIE *looks over at* MANCE—*then back to* DR COUSA.
We focus on restoring balance—we use nutrition—diet—all right, we use treatments that include B-17, a

form of Laetrile—a product derived from the pits of apricots—OK—I will not expound here—but this theory was first introduced by a Chinese herbalist in the year 2800 BC—OK?! It is cyanide containing substance—a nitriloside—and there continues to be a lack of consistent standards in its production. You see?! But this is secondary, because the reversal process must start in our hearts, in our hearts and our minds.

> DR COUSA *steps over to* MANCE, *putting his arm around him.*

Mance has had to change everything—*everything.*

EDDIE: Everything huh?!

DR COUSA: Top to bottom, start to finish.

EDDIE: Hmmm.

DR COUSA: He has had to change everything—he has had to change the very way he perceives the world, how he reacts to this world. [*beats*] The transformation must take place throughout the entire organism, not just in the aberrant cells, not just in the tumors.

> EDDIE *and* DR COUSA *watch each other. Pause.* DR FRENCH *steps toward* EDDIE...

DR FRENCH: The organism must not abuse itself anymore.

EDDIE: Uh huh.

DR FRENCH: Everything here is done to promote health and cleanliness.

> DR FRENCH *now stands next to* EDDIE...

Would you like anything? Some orange juice?

EDDIE: Nothing. Thanks.

DR COUSA: Moderation. [*beats*] Excess in anything leads to distortions, to deformities.

DR FRENCH *backs away...*

DR FRENCH: I must go. A pleasure Eddie.

EDDIE *nods as* DR FRENCH *exits.*

MANCE: Can you move me out of the sun.

DR COUSA: Of course.

DR COUSA *moves wheelchair a few feet to the left. Silence.*

EDDIE: No cancer in animals... well I remember my cocker spaniel died of fuck'n cancer.

DR COUSA: [*to* EDDIE] No spontaneous cancer. [*turning to* MANCE] How is the pain today Mance?

MANCE: It's much the same.

EDDIE: Spontaneous cancer huh.

DR COUSA *looks at* EDDIE—*pause.*

DR COUSA: 1971–September one, 1971, the FDA announced, after an ad-hoc committee of experts, and so on–they said that Laetrile may not be tested or sold in the United States, under provisions of the Federal Food, Drug, and Cosmetic Act. I had to leave the country. First I went to the Dominican Republic, then Bermuda, and finally Mexico. [*pause*] An "ad-hoc committee"... [*beats*] Are you going to tell me something new Edward?

EDDIE *stands and then slowly turns away. Silence.*
I have to make rounds.

He leans in to MANCE.

[*pause*] Beautiful day isn't it?!

MANCE: The water. The water looks almost emerald today.

DR COUSA *nods, smiles, backing away, exiting.*
EDDIE *steps over to* MANCE. *Silence. Lights dim until only small area around* MANCE *and* EDDIE *is lit.*

The gulf of California—or, as it's called, the Sea of Cortez. [*pause*] The history is full of Jesuits—disease—the occasional hurricane. [*pause*] They grow dates out there, and olives.—They got a federal prison here someplace, but it's got no prisoners at the moment. Good sportfishing—a few American college students on the weekend. [*pause*] It's too late for me to have much time on my hands. Even waiting to die, too much time can be a problem. [*pause*] My whole life, I've never been close to anybody when they died. I'd always hear about it later, my mom—I heard about it months later... and my dad, I just assume he's dead [*laughs then coughs—pause*]... He was an immigrant—the low class old fuck and he'd beat whoever was available, and I can only hope he died a miserable, slow, painful death.

EDDIE: You ever hear anybody say anything good abut you Mance?

MANCE: Not to my face.

    EDDIE *smiles. Pause.*

EDDIE: There's nothing happening out there. [*beat*] See?! [*beats*] And I turned forty last year—and things are slow... it's just very slow...

MANCE: Slow. [*nods slowly*]

EDDIE: ...And I figure you owe me something... Mance? What do you figure? Huh? You think I deserve something?

MANCE: You can't find anyone who doesn't deserve more of something.

EDDIE: ...But I think maybe my situation, you know, needs a second look.

MANCE: All right.

EDDIE: All right. [*beat*] Talk about my lack of prospects. [*getting angry*] My prospects—see—prospects is a thing I never had. So, so let's discuss why you never tried to be any help?

MANCE: Help you with what?

Pause.

EDDIE: I tell you I lived in Michigan—? The upper Peninsula.

MANCE *turns and stares at him. Silence.*

Never told you about that I guess. [*pause*] Job scene there sort of fell apart—after a while. [*pause*] I looked up Malone when I got to California. [*pause*] He's the one told me you were here.

Lights up slowly on the FORTUNE TELLER *and* TRANSLATOR. *As* EDDIE *continues we hear* FORTUNE TELLER *stuttering softly.*

FORTUNE TELLER: ah, ah, ah, ah, ah, ah, ah, ah, ah, ah, ah…

EDDIE *and* MANCE *continue simultaneously…*

EDDIE: I was a dispatcher—in Michigan—I did pretty well, 'til the cutbacks began—I mean, among these guys I was a lot quicker—smarter—quicker to pick up things and so I got a "supervisional" position—

FORTUNE TELLER *now mumbles to* TRANSLATOR, *then stutters again, more emphatically…*

FORTUNE TELLER: Ch, ch, ch, ch, ch, ch, ch, ch…

As EDDIE *and* MANCE *continue…*

EDDIE: All the money has just leaked out of those towns. Towns that have stopped repairing broken street lights—potholes—anything.

FORTUNE TELLER: [*louder*] Ch, ch, ah, ch, ah, chee, chee, chee, chee, chee, chee, chee, chee, chee...

MANCE: What? Eddie? Speak up...

FORTUNE TELLER: [*loudly now*] Ah, ah, ah, ah, ah, ah, ah, ah...

EDDIE: So I looked up Malone. Malone was in the phone book—[*pause*] But Malone isn't much help.

MANCE: What?

FORTUNE TELLER: [*loudly*] Ah, ah, ah, ah, ah, ah, ah, ah...

EDDIE: Malone wants to watch you die—

MANCE: What?

EDDIE: Malone wants to be here, wants to watch you die.

FORTUNE TELLER: Ah, ah, ah, ah, ah, ah, ah, ah...

MANCE: Eddie...? What did you say?

> *Lights fading out on* EDDIE *and* MANCE.

Eddie?

> *Lights out—Lights remain up on* FORTUNE TELLER *and* TRANSLATOR. *She turns out toward audience...*

TRANSLATOR: When it comes, Eddie, it comes in a gentle voice... Eddie?

> *She opens hands—palms up.*

[*pause*] For the saints, please... Eddie... [*beats*] to make the whispering stop. [*beats*] Eddie...

> FORTUNE TELLER *mumbles to her...*

To soothe the dreams... [*beats*] for your dreams... Eddie?...

> *Lights fade out.*

Lights up. MALONE *and* MANCE *in pool of light.*

MALONE: What can you see?

MANCE: I can't see much.

MALONE: [*nods*] You can see me.

MANCE: I know who it is.

MALONE: Can you see my face?

MANCE: [*beats*] I see better in daylight.

MALONE: It gets very fuck'n dark down here at night.
    Silence.

MANCE: Twice before—I've almost died. [*beats*] Thirty-three years ago, the first time.

MALONE: In the desert.

MANCE: I was shot in the head.

MALONE: It was the bleeding. They said you almost died—it was how much blood you lost.

MANCE: The second time was fifteen years ago—I had pneumonia, [*pause*] I was young then, I did not believe that man would shoot me.

MALONE: Anyone can shoot you. They have the gun—they pull the trigger. There is no doubt about this.

MANCE: I had dreamed of my death before—since I was a boy. And leading up to my being shot, the dreams became more frequent. [*pause*] Then there it was—and there was no pain. And I never had those dreams again.
    Pause.

MALONE: Eight, ten, years since I seen you.

MANCE: This time there's pain.

MALONE: They'll carry you out of here—at sunset—they'll place that wreath on your right side—a bunch of white carnations. [*beats*] They got carnations down here?

MANCE: I don't know.

MALONE: They'll bury you one morning—before it gets too hot. [*beats*] And I'll try to find you some carnations, and I might be the only guy there who knows you.

MANCE: [*pause*] You're a fool. [*pause*] All the years I've known you…

Silence.

Lights fade out.

Lights up on EDDIE *and* FORTUNE TELLER *and* TRANSLATOR.

EDDIE *stands—looking at both of them.*

EDDIE: In the first of these I was chasing some rats down the street. It was night, and the streets were wet, and it felt cold. The rats were big, and there were dozens of them. And as I ran faster I suddenly noticed a snake alongside me—and he was chasing the rats too—slithering down the street—and then there were no more lights, and I was running through the dark—and then I fell, and I was rolling and could feel the snake was caught up with me, and we were rolling together and then we came to a stop. And I was breathing hard—each breath was hard—hard. And I felt I was becoming part snake, and I stood up, and I was feeling some panic, and looked around, and I saw my reflection in the glass door and I saw the skin on my face had started to form scales and I had caught the rat, and swallowed it, and the rat's tail was hanging out of my nostril—moving back and forth and I woke up screaming.

Lights fade out.

Lights up on veranda. RUSS *seated, blanket over his lap.* MALONE *stands,* MANCE *in wheelchair.*

MALONE: All the money we made—and nothin's left. [*pause*] Massage parlors, adult books, mail order—but things changed... the times changed...

    Silence.

MANCE: [*pause*] You think I owe you some money?

MALONE: That's what I think.

    MANCE *nods slowly. Silence.*

MANCE: That's a long time ago.

MALONE: I didn't come for any money. That's not why I came. [*pause*] You owe me, but I don't want anything.

MANCE: All right.

    Pause.

MALONE: Back when I worked for you—we did a lot of the same things—did a lot of things together. [*beats*] Somehow I ended up broke—and you just kept making money. I wanted to understand that part.

    Silence, MANCE *moves forward—looking out over balustrade toward the sea.*

MANCE: The ruins of a Jesuit mission are out at the end of the road there. It was built in the early seventeen hundreds. The Jesuits failed, riddled with epidemics—their Indian slaves died by the thousands. The Franciscans failed later—under Junipero Serra. Same problems.

    Pause.

Really, there was never much here. [*pause*] This was still federal territory until about seventy-four—didn't become a state until then. [*beat*] Nobody cared enough about it.

> RUSS *stands, folds blanket and puts it on chair.*

MALONE: I have no friends left—Mance—everyone's gone, everyone's dead.

> MANCE *looks at him.* RUSS *exits as lights fade on* MALONE *and* MANCE.

> *Lights follow* RUSS *to hospital room with* DR COUSA *and* DR FRENCH. EDDIE *enters from opposite side.*

DR COUSA: Russ… Eddie… please, please…

> DR COUSA *ushers* RUSS *over to bed where he sits, and* EDDIE *to chair.* EDDIE *sits.*

There… Eddie…

> DR COUSA *looking down at* EDDIE.

Out late, Edward.

EDDIE: Is it?

> DR COUSA *turns to* RUSS.

DR COUSA: You having trouble sleeping?

RUSS: Yes, yes I am.

DR COUSA: Hmmm… sleep can be a mysterious phenomenon.

> DR COUSA *nods, smiles, goes back to* RUSS…

Russ has never slept well. His mother troubled his sleep—she would wake him to tell him about her problems, her anxieties.

> DR COUSA *pats* RUSS *on shoulder.*

RUSS: I had to listen.

DR COUSA: Often until the first light of morning.

RUSS: I had to listen—sitting up in bed.

DR COUSA: She'd tell him all her current fears, her angers, the chronic jealousies and hatred that shadowed her through each day.

RUSS: She'd sit in her bed–watching television until there were no more shows on, and then she'd sit in the dark until she couldn't stand it and she would come downstairs to my room and sit on the edge of my bed and shake me until I awoke and she would begin to recite these difficulties she saw–and I would sit up– and I'd listen–waiting for the sky to lighten–through a crack in the curtains in my room–I'd keep looking over to see if the darkness had started to lift...because when it would begin to lift I knew she would return to her room, and she would sleep.

DR COUSA *moves over toward* EDDIE...

DR COUSA: Edward... I've noted, that often, new surroundings can occasion a disruption in normal sleep patterns. [*pause*] But you say that's not the case with you.

EDDIE: I sleep fine.

DR COUSA: Well–isn't that fortunate.

EDDIE: Uh huh.

DR COUSA: [*pause*] Not everyone can be cured. That just isn't a reasonable expectation.

EDDIE: Doesn't seem like, no.

DR COUSA: I do not work miracles.

Silence.

Sometimes people think, they expect, the impossible. [*pause*] And when they receive disappointment they become embittered–and even vengeful.

DR COUSA *turns away–looks at* DR FRENCH, *then at* RUSS, *then back to* EDDIE.

It's getting very late Ed—and you know, you can't make up for lost sleep.

EDDIE *stands...*

EDDIE: I didn't know that.

DR COUSA: You may try to sleep a little extra the next day—but it doesn't work—once it's lost, it's lost.

EDDIE: What?—the hours?

DR COUSA *puts his arm around him—*

DR COUSA: You should try to go to sleep before you tire too much.

They walk downstage together, slowly...

It's the hours before midnight—that's the sleep you need the most.

They stop.

Edward, I know the sort of young man that you are—I know the things that haunt you—[*pause*] when you walk you have the look of hunted game. [*beat*] That nervousness—the 'You can't hit a moving target' kinetic swagger. [*beat*] I know the violent daydreams you carry within you—the silent curses you mouth to yourself.

Silence.

I've seen hundreds of young men like you. [*pause*] Take some time Edward, and think of the road you're traveling. [*beats*] I can tell you where those other young men ended up. Men who resembled you in many ways—men who lived much as you have—without guidance, without direction—men, young men, from broken homes. [*beats*] I can tell you of the tragedy, but I think you know already. [*pause*] Don't you?

DR COUSA *smiles benevolently.*

I don't expect an answer, Edward. Not now. I only want you to think back over what I've said, how I've spoken to you.

EDDIE *nods, and he backs away. The lights fade on* DR COUSA *and come up on* FORTUNE TELLER *and* TRANSLATOR. FORTUNE TELLER *begins to stutter, more frenetically than before. The* TRANSLATOR *moves imploringly toward* EDDIE...

TRANSLATOR: You are afraid.

EDDIE *hesitates, standing just outside the light.*

FORTUNE TELLER: [*continuing*] Ah, ah, ah, ah, ah, ah...

TRANSLATOR: Closer... Eddie...

EDDIE *takes a single step closer.*

FORTUNE TELLER: [*continues*] Ch, ch, ch, ch, ch, ch, ch, ch, ch, ch...

TRANSLATOR: You want protection?!

EDDIE: [*almost under his breath*] The fuck are you sayin'?

EDDIE *inches backward—then has impulse to move forward—but stops.*

FORTUNE TELLER: Ah, ah, ah, ah, ah, ah, ah, ah, ah, ah...

TRANSLATOR: Give him your hand...

EDDIE *steps forward—*

Open it...

She extends her hand—palm up—to show EDDIE. Here, Eddie, open.

EDDIE *stares at them.*

FORTUNE TELLER: [*softer*] Ch, ch, ch, ch, ch, ch, ch, ch, ch, ch...

TRANSLATOR: With your palms lifted—with your palms open—

Pause—EDDIE *doesn't move.*

FORTUNE TELLER: [*softly*] Ch, ch, ch, ch, ch, ch, ch, ch, ch, ch...

TRANSLATOR: Is there anything you want to ask?

> EDDIE *remains silent.* FORTUNE TELLER *stops.*
> *She slowly takes hold of his hands—she hold them...*

Your hands are cold.

> *He pulls them away.*

FORTUNE TELLER: Ch, ch, ch, ch, ch, ch, ch...

TRANSLATOR: What do you want to ask? [*beats*] You have to ask... [*beat*] only to ask...

> EDDIE *backing away as lights fade out.*

> *Lights up slowly on* MANCE. EDDIE *stands behind him.*

EDDIE: First time I met you—she walked me in, holding my hand—then shoved me forward. I was maybe seven—eight. [*beats*] You showed me the scar on your head—where you were shot. [*pause*] It was still pretty fresh and pretty ugly—and I had nightmares about that for a long time.

> MANCE *smiles without warmth. Silence.*

You laughed at me—'cause it was pretty funny that I was scared. You said it was nothing to have a hole in your head—asked me "did I want a little hole in my head—right above my ear."

> MANCE *laughs—short—hoarse. Silence.*

I started crying. That's the most I ever cried about anything. The most scared I ever been.

> *Lights fade out.*

Spot up MANCE *in wheelchair. Alone.*

MANCE: I dream of mermaids. [*pause*] It's night—on the sea—virgins—quietly—afloat on the glassy black water. [*pause*] And I want my body tossed from the bow of a steamship—in the dead of night, meeting the water in a splash I'll never hear.

Lights fade out.

Lights up on EDDIE *standing downstage.* RUSS *is behind him. In rear is* DR COUSA *puffing a large cigar.*

EDDIE: Can I tell you something?

Silence.

Ross—it's Ross isn't it?

RUSS: [*nods slightly*] Russ.

EDDIE: I'll tell you this—you see, I'm not a real passive kind of person. [*pause*] I did not grow up with a real positive outlook and I do not "deal" well—you see what I'm sayin' ?!

Silence.

I do not have a family.

Pause.

I'm not a weakling. I know how to take care of myself.

EDDIE *leans in closer...*

I'm not someone to play with. I am not a play-mate. [*beat*] I believe a man should learn how to take care of himself.

EDDIE *pulls back.*

[*with sarcastic edge*] You got somewhere you got to be—? I don't want to keep you from anything.

RUSS: I have no place I have to go.

EDDIE: OK—good.

RUSS: [*pause*] I would like to go home. [*beats*] Eventually.

EDDIE: You would huh?!

RUSS: I had a twin. My twin brother. [*pause*] This is a story. About my brother.

EDDIE: Hmmm.

RUSS: He would complain—this is how it began—he would complain of bad headaches. Then of blurred vision. His face twitched—around the eyes and his behavior changed. He did not seem like my brother anymore. Then he died. He had a pituitary tumor. [*pause*] My family sent me away to school after that. I was twenty-one.

EDDIE: That's the story?

RUSS: Jerome was sickly his whole life.

Pause as they look at each other.

EDDIE: How long you been here?

Lights up on DR COUSA—*still puffing cigar.*

DR COUSA: I read the report from Queens General— New York. Severe headaches and progressive loss of vision. Originally diagnosed as chiasmal lesion. The visual fields diminished—more severely in the left. Cerebro angiogram revealed a mass in the fronto-parietal area—a meningioma—explaining the psychotic episodes. X-rays of skull show curvilinear radiolucent defect in frontal region.

Angiography: the anterior cerebral artery radically displaced—[*pause*] it went on, pathology in the optic foramina and then the twitching of right facialis—

strong and often painful. [*pause*] Brain tumor—. And so he died. He was twenty-one.

Silence. He walks downstage. Lights crossfade—
EDDIE. TRANSLATOR *stands silently.* FORTUNE TELLER *sits.*

EDDIE: [*angrily*] No—no—uh huh—listen kitten—I dreamed—I had a dream—of you—I just now—only just now—I dreamed I was fucking you—and it wasn't very good—but I was fucking you—and I kept fucking you— I was fucking you hard and when I looked at you— you were a lot of people I knew—and I looked away and there was a mirror and I saw myself and I had no arm—just a crudely stitched stump and my whole body and face were deep red—maroon—and my hair was turning black—but then I noticed my hand hanging in mid-air—just where it would be if I'd still had my arm—and it wasn't burned, it was white—and it seemed to gesture to me, and then I woke—I couldn't breathe.

Silence. Lights follow EDDIE *to rear, seated downstage is* DR COUSA.

DR COUSA: [*to* EDDIE] A renowned physician once said "Internal medicine was born of witchcraft—and surgery the child of the battlefield." [*pause*] You know the saying—"the horse would have lived except it died." [*beats*] Perhaps it's just a crap shoot. What do you think?

Silence. Lights fade out very slowly.
End of Act I

ACT 2

In darkness—sound of wind—loud, stormy—intense. A small light comes up on EDDIE *—very gradually. He is squatting—darkness all around him. After a couple moments* EDDIE *lights a cigarette. After another couple moments the sound of wind/storm fades slightly and another light comes up revealing* MANCE, *in wheelchair, blanket on his lap. The sound continues throughout scene. He watches* EDDIE *a moment.*

MANCE: You should think about quitting.

> EDDIE *looks over at him.* MANCE *laughs, a raspy laugh that turns into a cough. Finally he stops. Silence.* EDDIE *looks back out at the water.*

Have you heard any forecasts? Anything about the weather?

EDDIE: Nothing.

MANCE: About the storm?

EDDIE: I didn't hear anything.

MANCE: Hurricane. [*beats*] Moving north from the equator. [*pause*] More than one storm will form at times—both moving north.

EDDIE: I haven't heard anything.

MANCE: Very little protection—this area—from the hurricanes.

EDDIE: [*pause*] Shit's in Spanish here—I don't understand it.

MANCE: [*pause*] "Course not." [*pause*] This is hurricane
season, in this part of the world. [*beats*] Tropical
storms, tropical depressions, tropical cyclones, hurricanes. On the horizon, the layers of cumulus
clouds—cumulonimbus, walling off the true storm—
you can see the rain bands first—and feel the air
change. Storms are natural forces—they gestate, are
given birth and grow—from adolescence to maturity,
and eventually death. Decline and death. A tropical
storm cannot form exactly on the equator—they must
be ten or fifteen degrees from it—where the earth's
rotation can nuture their destructiveness. [*pause*] The
peoples of hurricane prone areas, they live in fear
during the warm season—they never sleep well, and
authorities have documented the increase in domes-
tic quarrels, public intoxication, traffic accidents. The
collective life of the people vibrates at a higher pitch—
the nervous system is affected, headaches are common, and auditory impairment often occurs. [*pause*]
Western Pacific storms tend to be shorter lived than
Atlantic systems. In 1939 I'm told, in September, September '39, five separate hurricanes struck Baja California. The most famous came ashore at Ensenada—
it moved up across San Diego. They called the storm
"El Cordonazo"—the lash of St. Francis. [*beats*] Beautiful isn't it—the lash of St. Francis.

    Long silence.

I did very little traveling, most of my life—didn't grasp
the idea—never thought about vacations. [*pause*] I
never came here, to Mexico. [*pause*] Business took
up all of my time. [*beats*] The films, the massage par-

lors, mail order. My business concerns. [*pause*] My warehouse employed eleven men. Eleven. All of the boxing up and shipping adult magazines. Magazines, newspapers, catalogues. I needed two lawyers just to keep track of where I sent what—which states had passed new obscenity rulings—which didn't care, and who could be bought. I mailed to every state in the country at one time or another. [*beat*] The climate changed—by the mid-seventies I had to close down all the shipping and mail order. [*beat*] Do you remember this magazine—very small—"God" I believe, that's what it was called—this magazine—the name of the magazine; it was "God". I don't recall how many issues came out—not many. There was a lot of "excrement eating"—and some child porn—pictures—and then addresses of those child/love enthusiasts. "God" was a kind of test—to push things—see how far you could go.

> MANCE *looks at* EDDIE—*silence.* MANCE *laughs to himself—coughs.* EDDIE *looks back at him.*

I think we could have gotten away with the eating shit, but the pictures of little eight and nine year olds, spreading their legs provocatively, striking sexy poses, licking their lips and touching themselves—that's where the line was drawn. That created considerable pressure.

> *Pause.*

EDDIE: It's disgusting.

MANCE: [*beats*] Yes, of course it is.

> EDDIE *stands. He looks around. Finally he turns, looking at* MANCE.

MALONE: Nevada, if memory serves. The majority of child pornography came from Nevada. Small enclaves of boy-man love, or man-girl, all kinds of combinations and specialities. Little communities devoted almost entirely to their specific erotic pursuits. [*beats*] Out in the nowhere of the Great Basin, alongside the survivalist outposts, the random casino or copper mine.

EDDIE: They're disgusting.

MANCE: Who?

EDDIE: People who do that stuff.

MANCE *looks at him, says nothing.*

Makes me sick. All of it. The sleaze, all of it.

MANCE: Makes you feel dirty.

EDDIE: [*beats*] I just never liked any of it. [*pause*] I never liked fuck films, looking at dirty pictures. I just didn't ever do those things.

MANCE: You were raised correctly. [*beats*] Isn't that it?

EDDIE: [*pause*] The worst is with kids. [*pause*] I just never liked it.

MANCE: [*beats*] Makes you angry.

EDDIE *stares at him a moment...*

EDDIE: [*nodding*] Makes me angry. [*pause*] I don't know how people can do things like that.

MANCE: [*silence*] I'm sure you don't.

MANCE *stares at him. Silence. Sound of wind/ storm increases gradually as lights slowly fade.*

Lights up slowly. DR COUSA—*slowly getting dressed— putting on a long sleeved white shirt.* DR FRENCH *sits, watching. Silence.*

DR FRENCH: I hate the way mold grows on everything. [*pause*] Everywhere. Everything.

> DR COUSA *is buttoning his shirt–taking great care with his appearance. He is slipping on his rings– checking his hair–the last touches.*

You can't live as a white man. Not here.

> *Pause.*

DR COUSA: There are times when I imagine a home— my home, a home to return to. [*beats*] But there is none. I can return nowhere.

> *Lights come up downstage, revealing* EDDIE *wheeling in* MANCE. DR COUSA *and* DR FRENCH *approach...*

On the beach this morning. [*beats*] The tide is already washing out the low lying housing. [*pause*] By to-morrow... who knows? Right? Might wash away everything.

> DR COUSA *smiles, laughs.* DR COUSA *stands close to* MANCE...

[*softly to* MANCE] I wish you'd come to me sooner.

> MANCE *nods slowly.*

Before the chemotherapy, before all the drugs–before the "cancer industry" had begun to destroy your inner life.

> *After a moment,* DR COUSA *straightens up, looking over at* EDDIE...

It's all about money–that's what it's all about.

EDDIE: [*beat*] What "what" is all about?

DR COUSA: [*beat*] Everything–the destruction of life.

> EDDIE *stares at him. Silence.* DR COUSA *takes a deep breath.*

The air is changing.

> DR COUSA *takes another deep breath. Lights slowly fade as* EDDIE *backs away, with* DR FRENCH...
>
> *Light on:* EDDIE *and* DR FRENCH...

DR FRENCH: You're losing your hair.

> EDDIE *touches his receding hairline...*

You don't have to. [*beats*] I was involved in various cosmetic surgeries—I personally performed over three thousand hair restoration procedures.

EDDIE: I'm not too concerned. [*beat*] People go bald—right? Happens.

DR FRENCH: [*nodding*] ... Hair transplantation works. [*pause*] Virtually painless. [*beats*] Bottom fell out of hair restoration and I had my reasons. [*beat*] When I left—I had good reasons.

> *Pause.*

EDDIE: Mance is gonna die soon. [*pause*] Anyone come here who doesn't die?

DR FRENCH: People come here who are terminal... otherwise they don't come.

EDDIE: Last resort.

DR FRENCH: The very last.

EDDIE: But nobody is ever really cured?

DR FRENCH: "Cured" is a vague word. [*beat*] Everybody dies.

> *Silence.*

EDDIE: You work with only the very desperate—right? [*beats*] The very desperate.

> DR FRENCH *only looks at him. Pause.* EDDIE *takes a couple steps back...*

I'm goin' back to the hotel. I gotta pay another day.
[*beats*] Pay by the day.

> EDDIE *looks at* DR FRENCH. *Lights fade out.*
> *In dark: Sound of storm.*

> *Lights up slowly. Storm fades out gradually.*
> MALONE *standing—holding up umbrella.* EDDIE
> *huddled against wall in background.*

MALONE: The road's closed. Washed out.

EDDIE: You want to go back to L.A.?

MALONE: [*beat*] Yes I do.

EDDIE: We're paid up 'til Sunday.

> MALONE *nods. Pause.*

MALONE: I've seen him. [*pause—shrugs contemptuously*]
He's a dead man. [*pause*] I've seen him.

EDDIE: [*beat*] OK.

MALONE: You should come with me. [*beat*] Let him die
alone.

> *Silence.*

EDDIE: When she got sick… [*pause*] Nobody ever told
me.

MALONE: I don't know about that.

EDDIE: She was cremated?!

MALONE: Yeah.

EDDIE: Some service, they scattered her ashes. They
phoned me—asked did I want them scattered over
the sea, over the desert, or over the mountains. [*beats*]
I said the sea. [*beat*] Probably, those guys, they probably just put the ashes, just put them in some
dumpster—out in the alley.

MALONE: No way to know for sure.

EDDIE: I read about this place—this funeral home—they just burnt all these bodies together, all mixed up—to save time, save money—and they'd just divvie up the ashes—this much in this can—this much in this one.

MALONE: [*shrugs*] Lots of unscrupulous folks out there.

EDDIE: Yeah, I guess there are.

Pause.

MALONE: Why'd you choose the sea?

EDDIE: What?

MALONE: Why'd you choose to have her ashes scattered on the sea?

EDDIE: I don't know.

MALONE: I don't remember her liking the ocean—anything like that. [*beat*] She hated the beach.

EDDIE: [*pause*] I don't know.

MALONE *nods slowly. Sound of storm increases...*

MALONE: I want to leave here.

Long silence.

Your mother lived with me first. It was never like that for her again. [*pause*] It was something else altogether, her life with Mance. [*pause*] She didn't have a regular life with him.

Pause. EDDIE *steps forward.*

EDDIE: Is that what she had with you? A regular life?

They look at each other.

'Cause you're such a regular guy?!

Sound of storm becoming even louder. Pause.

MALONE: She didn't leave me for Mance—you know that?! There were other men.

EDDIE: If you say so. What's the difference...?!

MALONE: By the time the Mance thing happened...

[*pause*] You were pretty little... [*pause*] I didn't know your Dad. [*pause*] I don't know that much about it—the way it started...what she was thinking.

EDDIE: [*beats*] I never figured you knew anything.

MALONE: [*pause*] You're too old to ask anyone for help Eddie. At your age, you're not sympathetic.

> *Lights fade out.*
>
> *Lights up slowly on:* EDDIE, *alone in front of* FORTUNE TELLER'S *stall. He looks around—silence. Crossfade lights—out on* EDDIE, *slowly up on* DR COUSA. *He sits, after a moment he looks over his shoulder...*

DR COUSA: Eddie.

> EDDIE *steps forward into the light. Pause.*

They may have left. [*beats*] This kind of storm, it just screws up everything.

> *They look at each other. Pause.*

Most of our power is out. Already.

EDDIE: [*beat*] Left where?

DR COUSA: Huh? Ah... I couldn't tell you. [*pause*] The American authorities are going to come for me—won't be long. A few more months—maybe less. [*beats*] Fraud, and... who knows what else. FBI, and the FDA, the National Cancer Institute—they'll all be starting to formulate their cases now—deciding how to prosecute.

EDDIE: You going to move?

DR COUSA: [*pause*] I'll move, yes.

EDDIE: Where?

> DR COUSA *shrugs. Silence.*

And what happens to your patients?

DR COUSA: They'll go somewhere else. [*pause*] Why do you stay Eddie, why not leave? [*beats*] Maybe it's what you're going back to?! That what scares you?

EDDIE: You think I'm scared.

DR COUSA: What you're asking from Mance...? You're asking him; can I return to you? [*pause*] It would be best, be easier, after he's dead. Don't you think?

> DR FRENCH *steps forward into the light. He has on sleeveless undershirt. He's just taken a shower and is drying his hair. He watches* EDDIE *and* DR COUSA...

How old are you? Huh? People will look at you... People you know. You're not a kid anymore—and when they look at you, at what you do, at your lack of plans, your lack of goals... they think; such a pity, if he could have only found a direction—something to which he could apply himself... [*pause*] Such a waste... it's really too bad. Friends will want to avoid your having contact with their children—you're not a good example, not a good influence. [*beats*] Things have changed, for those friends, they have families— they've grown up—and they won't want to be reminded of when they were like you... but that was when we were younger they'll tell each other—and now we've changed—we know where we're going. [*beats*] They don't want you around, Eddie, things can't be careless and unpredictable any longer. They'll think of themselves as responsible now, as moral— and you'll just be another of those unattached men who they experience as threatening—as sick.

Silence. EDDIE *steps backward... as lights change—crossfade, out on* DR COUSA *and* DR FRENCH. *Lights coming up on* MANCE *in bed,* RUSS *sits next to bed.* EDDIE *stands, watching.* RUSS *has open book on his lap—he looks up at* EDDIE. MANCE *lies on his back, asleep.*

RUSS: I'm reading to him. [*beats*] I'm reading him Thucydides.

　　　EDDIE *pulls up chair and sits next to* RUSS.

EDDIE: He's sleeping.

RUSS: [*pause*] I usually keep reading. He'll wake...and fall asleep. Wake and fall asleep, several times in an hour.

EDDIE: You like doing this?

RUSS: Reading?

EDDIE: You like reading, here, this way, to this old man?

　　　Sound of FORTUNE TELLER *stuttering.* RUSS *listens a moment, then looks at* EDDIE...

RUSS: I can't read anymore now, the electricity—we have to conserve on the generator.

　　　EDDIE *stands. Pause.*

Because of the rain. The rain and the storm.

　　　Lights crossfading as stuttering continues. EDDIE *walks downstage into light as lights fade on* RUSS *and* MANCE. *The* TRANSLATOR *is there, alone. The stuttering continues throughout scene.*

TRANSLATOR: Eddie...

EDDIE: I've had a third dream.

TRANSLATOR: Money, Eddie, for protection.

　　　He stares at her. She extends her hand.

For shelter. Please.

EDDIE: I want to tell you the dream. I want to tell you both the dream.

Sound of storm added to stuttering. Both increasing...

TRANSLATOR: Everything has closed down Eddie. There are no more fortunes...

EDDIE: You were in my dream.

TRANSLATOR: Money, please. You must give.

EDDIE digs in his pocket—brings out a single dollar.

EDDIE: This is my last dollar.

He shoves it toward her angrily.

I'm broke now—that's it.

She takes it and starts backing away.

TRANSLATOR: We are left out in the storm. [*beat*] You and me...all of us...

In background light starts coming up on DR COUSA. He stands watching EDDIE and TRANSLATOR. Lights slowly fading out on downstage area.

EDDIE: Wait.

TRANSLATOR: You must give, for the saints, for the future, to find shelter... to fight the pain...

Lights out.

Lights up slowly, on MANCE sitting up in bed. Sound of storm fades very gradually out. DR COUSA stands next to him.

MANCE: Is it night?

DR COUSA: It's evening.

MANCE nods. Silence. He looks at DR COUSA.

MANCE: You have any children?

DR COUSA: No.

MANCE: Any wives?

DR COUSA: No. None.

MANCE: I have no children.

DR COUSA: I did not want any children.

MANCE: Fatherhood as an idea always felt unsavory to
    me. [*pause*] You produce boys, and you must wait
    for them to try and destroy who you are—and fathers
    with their daughters, fathers and their growing girls,
    that is an ever spreading infection, a sunless tunnel
    of filth and cowardice.

> Pause, then MANCE *hacks out a laugh... which
> eventually becomes a prolonged cough.*

[*pause*] I feel my body disappearing.

DR COUSA: Within all men, the capacity exists to fall
    sick. It is the potential of all living tissue.

MANCE: [*pause*] I've never trusted anyone.

DR COUSA: Uh huh.

MANCE: And nobody has ever trusted me.

DR COUSA: You made a great deal of money Mance, in
    your lifetime.

MANCE: A great deal.

DR COUSA: Is that what Eddie wants?

> *Silence.*

MANCE: I made my money selling pornography... and I
    spent my money on much the same thing... on sex—
    on things like sex—always with strangers. What I have
    left I'm spending with you. [*pause*] I don't believe in
    having anything to do sexually with people I know
    too well. It embarrasses me. It embarrasses both of
    us.

> *Silence.*

DR COUSA: The FDA is trying to find a reason—the FBI—Mexico is no longer safe for me.

MANCE: I'll try to hurry and die. [*laughs hoarsely*] I won't linger.

> DR COUSA *looks at him.*
>
> *Lights come up further revealing* DR FRENCH *who strolls forward. He has on white lab coat. He pauses, then gives* MANCE *a big smile...*

DR FRENCH: Well, Mance, you about ready for some dinner?

MANCE: If you like.

DR FRENCH: I'll tell the girls in the kitchen—I'll tell Russ to bring it up to you. How's that sound?

> MANCE *looks at* DR FRENCH, *then at* DR COUSA. *Pause.*

MANCE: Is there anyone else left? Besides me? Besides Russ?

DR COUSA: No one else.

DR FRENCH: Red snapper. Broiled with rice and beans. How's that sound?

MANCE: Red snapper. Hmmm.

DR COUSA: The FDA—the AMA—they persecute alternative treatment.

DR FRENCH: A little tomatillo sauce on the fish, and some sliced papaya—for dessert—sound OK to you?

MANCE: And a glass of water.

DR COUSA: People have the right to choose their own treatment. [*pause*] People have the right to self medication.

DR FRENCH: ...squeeze some lime on the papaya.

MANCE: Yes, lime, give it a little bite.

DR COUSA: The impurity of our lives is what kills us. I sometimes wonder if we couldn't live forever.

> DR FRENCH *is backing away as lights fade out.*

I believe it's possible... to live forever...

> *Sound of storm in dark.*

> *Dim spot up slowly on* MALONE. *Another light reveals* EDDIE *to side. Sound of storm fades a little but continues throughout the scene.* MALONE *starts humming, then singing "Walking My Baby Back Home"—the Johnny Ray version. After a moment he pauses, looks at* EDDIE *then sings a little more—this time* EDDIE *joins in for a couple bars. Then* MALONE *dances a few steps, sings, and finally stops. Pause.*

MALONE: Johnny Ray.

EDDIE: I know.

MALONE: That was a big hit for him. Everywhere you went you heard that tune. [*pause*] Your mother loved Johnny Ray.

EDDIE: She had the record. [*beats*] She played all his records.

> *Pause.*

MALONE: I can't drive—the road is washed out.

EDDIE: Johnny Ray wore a hearing aid. Did you know that? Called him Mr. Emotion.

MALONE: It was your mother liked him. I didn't care for him. She adored him. I told her he was a faggot... but she didn't care.

EDDIE: I remember all his songs.

MALONE: [*beat*] Me too. [*pause*] He was very big—very

big—for a couple years. Didn't last long. [*pause*] We weren't together then—it was after—but I'd still see her... I'd visit her once in awhile. I don't remember you—you had to have been pretty little.

EDDIE: I don't remember you then either... but then I was pretty little.

MALONE: Everywhere you went, you'd hear "Walkin' My Baby Back Home." [*beats*] Los Angeles wasn't big then—not the same kind of city it is now.

EDDIE: All my aunts—the only pictures I have—pictures of these parties with all my aunts. All her sisters.

MALONE: She had eight sisters.

EDDIE: She was the oldest. [*beat*] In the pictures the parties look pretty big. I don't even know the names of some of my aunts—nobody ever told me. I got their pictures though. One box of crummy photographs.

> MALONE *starts humming "Walkin' My Baby Back Home" quietly.*

[*pause*] I don't know why I looked you up.

> MALONE *singing now. Lights fade out as sound of storm increases. Sound of* FORTUNE TELLER *stuttering as sound of storm fades slightly. Light up gradually on* MANCE *in bed—stage center—another light up on* DR COUSA *nearby. A third light up slowly on* FORTUNE TELLER *seated alone. He keeps stuttering softly.*

DR COUSA: Adenocarcinoma of Sigmoid colon. [*beat*] Colon; extensively infiltrating and ulcerating anaplastic adenocarcinoma with evidence of metastasis of fatty mesocolon. [*pause*] Pinkish discharge with stools. Accumulation of gas and increasing difficulty in elimination of stools—mixed with bloody mucus and some pus. Original specialist found rectoscopy negative. Later x-rays found a filling defect ten inches above anus. [*beats*] Additionally patient complains of discomfort from old age arteriosclerosis.

>*Lights fading on* DR COUSA. *Moving behind* MANCE *is* DR FRENCH, *watching.*

MANCE: [*pause*] Is it night? Is it still night?

DR FRENCH: It's evening.

MANCE: [*pause*] I had mirrors on the walls. Had them installed myself, and one on the ceiling. [*beats*] I didn't do it to watch the women, I did it to watch myself.

DR FRENCH: [*pause*] Your supper is almost ready. [*beats*] I was just in the kitchen, the red snapper, well, there just are no words.

MANCE: I didn't want any photographs—nothing like that. [*beat*] When it was over I wasn't interested in reminiscences. Wasn't interested in the reliving of anything.

>*Lights fading out.*

>*Lights up on* EDDIE *standing near* FORTUNE TELLER *and* TRANSLATOR. *The* TRANSLATOR *steps toward* EDDIE...

TRANSLATOR: There are no more readings... no more fortunes told.

>EDDIE *says nothing. He doesn't seem to move. Pause.*

You have nothing to give?

>EDDIE *shakes head "no".*

I'm sorry Eddie.

EDDIE: I had another dream.

TRANSLATOR: It makes no difference.

> EDDIE *extends his hand, palm up...*

EDDIE: Have him look at my hand...

TRANSLATOR: We have been driven away.

EDDIE: I want him to look at my fuck'n hand...

> TRANSLATOR *backs away as lights start fading.*

TRANSLATOR: You have nothing Eddie... nothing... nothing... nothing... [*trailing off*]

> *Lights fade out.*
> *In dark, sound of storm.*

> *Spot up on* MALONE, *lit from neck up. Sound of storm fades only slightly.*

MALONE: Eddie...?

> *Light up slowly on* EDDIE *to side...*

[*pause*] The car's gone. [*beats*] I came back and it was gone.

EDDIE: The transmission is dead. It wouldn't run anyway.

MALONE: I'm soaked. Soaking wet... to the bone. [*beat*] Eddie?

EDDIE: What?

MALONE: Your mother—there were people who really cared about her.

EDDIE: That right?!

MALONE: [*pause*] Eddie... you know what I sometimes think? [*beat*] If I'd handled it all a little differently, with your mother—I think, I might have been able to do something to raise you.

EDDIE: Malone...

MALONE: I should have tried harder—with her—later—made a home for her, you know... and for you.

EDDIE: Malone? [*beats*] Fuck off... will you—just go and fuck off.

> *Lights going out on* EDDIE.

MALONE: Eddie? [*beats*] You can't understand...

> *Sound of storm increases as lights go out on* MALONE.

You can't know...

> *Lights out.*
> *In dark, sound of storm.*

> *Lights up slowly on* EDDIE, *standing, and* MANCE *in bed, on back. A plate of food on tray next to bed. Sound of storm fades slightly...*

EDDIE: It's a thing, what happens to your body.

> EDDIE *steps closer. Pause.*

I been sleeping in Malone's car, last couple of days. [*beats*] Seventy-five Mustang. [*pause*] I got no more money. [*beats*] Is Malone still here you ask? Ah, yeah, he's still around. He doesn't have anything left either. [*beats*] Looks like you didn't eat your dinner.

> EDDIE *bends over to look at plate of food.*

Fish, huh? [*pause*] You know, when I was a kid, I was kinda small—pretty small—in seventh grade I was almost the smallest kid in school. And I was always picked on. And I was afraid to fight back, 'cause I was so small I guess. And I stayed afraid. And I'm still afraid. I'm afraid of all kinds of shit—all the time. I'd like so much to not be afraid. To find a way to quit being scared.

MANCE *tries to speak but only wheezes. Pause.*
I was scared of you. [*pause*] Even at military school—
when you were a couple hundred miles away. I was
afraid of you. I'd be there and think of you—feel how
scared of you I was. [*pause*] I'm a grown man now.
    MANCE *wheezes again. Silence.*
You're gonna die tonight.
    EDDIE *picks up the plate of food.*
Looks pretty good—rice, beans—fish.
    He looks at MANCE, *leaning in close...*
Don't want to let it get cold.
    He dumps the food on MANCE, *half of it on his
face. He shoves it in his face. He straightens up.*
MANCE *shakes a little, wheezes.*
    Lights fade out.

    Spot up on DR COUSA *seated.* DR FRENCH *stands
a few feet behind him working on his hair...*
DR FRENCH: Russ has disappeared again.
DR COUSA: Hmmm.
DR FRENCH: He'll get lost... in this storm. I was won-
dering, thinking I might try Puerto Rico—try to get
into liposuction, fat farms... high end stuff.
    DR FRENCH *continues to primp.*
DR COUSA: Puerto Rico.
DR FRENCH: Puerto Rico. [*beats*] San Juan. [*beats*] The
Caribbean.
DR COUSA: [*beats*] Puerto Rico.
DR FRENCH: [*beats*] San Juan. [*beats*] A spa. A health
spa, sort of situation—specifically—what I was told.
[*pause*] A terrible rain.

DR COUSA: An intense rain. [*pause*] Twenty some years and I only find humiliation.

> *Lights fading on* DR COUSA *and* DR FRENCH *as* EDDIE *appears by* FORTUNE TELLER. *The* FORTUNE TELLER *looks at him but says nothing. The* TRANSLATOR *looks at him. Pause.*

EDDIE: In the third dream I was in a gymnasium. There were people there, but I couldn't tell if I knew them or not. [*indicating* TRANSLATOR] And you were there. The room had three windows—large windows. And through each window I could see a tornado approaching. The sky was dark, dark grey, very dark and the tornados were getting closer and then I felt the gymnasium moving—being blown along and I went to the window and it was black outside. And then I was clinging to the branches of a tree, you were holding on too, and we were being blown along this field— like a wheat field, but I wasn't—

> *Pin spot slowly up on* MAN *standing on platform—upstage center. We only see his legs from knee down. He has on same pants and shoes as opening of play.*

—afraid. Then we crashed into this small house—little two-story house, and the storm was over. I stood there with you, looking around. Then I saw this old woman looking down at us from a small window on the second story. She had a very neutral expression—she was just watching. All around my feet were vines with giant green cucumbers. My legs were entwined and I bent over and picked up one of the cucumbers and I cracked it open and it was full of thousand dollar bills. I dropped it and picked up another one and cracked it open. It was full of thousand dollar bills too. [*pause*] Then I woke up.

FORTUNE TELLER *starts to slowly stutter.* EDDIE *looks around helplessly. Lights fade out slowly on everything. Sound of storm increases. Blackout.*

END

JOHN STEPPLING

John Steppling has long been an important influence on theater in Southern California, particularly as the founder of theater companies and an original founding member of the Padua Hills Playwrights Festival. Among his many plays are *The Dream Coast, The Shaper, Standard of the Breed, Teenage Wedding, My Crummy Job, Deep Tropical Tan and Theory of Miracles,* and *Sea of Cortez.* A four-time NEA recipient for writing and directing, Steppling has also received a Rockefeller Fellowship, two *L.A. Weekly* Awards for Best Play, and a Pen-West award for drama. He also has written several screenplays and has traveled widely, recently living in Thailand for several months.

SUN & MOON CLASSICS

PIERRE ALFERI [France]
Natural Gaits 95 (1-55713-231-3, $10.95)
The Familiar Path of the Fighting Fish [in preparation]

CLAES ANDERSSON [Finland]
What Became Words 121 (1-55713-231-3, $11.95)

DAVID ANTIN [USA]
Death in Venice: Three Novellas [in preparation]
Selected Poems: 1963–1973 10 (1-55713-058-2, $13.95)

ECE AYHAN [Turkey]
A Blind Cat AND *Orthodoxies* [in preparation]

DJUNA BARNES [USA]
Ann Portuguise [in preparation]
The Antiphon [in preparation]
At the Roots of the Stars: The Short Plays 53 (1-55713-160-0, $12.95)
Biography of Julie von Bartmann [in preparation]
The Book of Repulsive Women 59 (1-55713-173-2, $6.95)
Collected Stories 110 (1-55713-226-7, $24.95 [cloth])
Interviews 86 (0-940650-37-1, $12.95)
New York 5 (0-940650-99-1, $12.95)
Smoke and Other Early Stories 2 (1-55713-014-0, $9.95)

CHARLES BERNSTEIN [USA]
Content's Dream: Essays 1975–1984 49 (0-940650-56-8, $14.95)
Dark City 48 (1-55713-162-7, $11.95)
Republics of Reality: 1975–1995 [in preparation]
Rough Trades 14 (1-55713-080-9, $10.95)

JENS BJØRNEBOE [Norway]
The Bird Lovers 43 (1-55713-146-5, $9.95)
Semmelweis [in preparation]

ANDRÉ DU BOUCHET [France]
The Indwelling [in preparation]
Today the Day [in preparation]
Where Heat Looms 87 (1-55713-238-0, $12.95)

ANDRÉ BRETON [France]
Arcanum 17 51 (1-55713-170-8, $12.95)
Earthlight 26 (1-55713-095-7, $12.95)

DAVID BROMIGE [b. England/Canada]
The Harbormaster of Hong Kong 32 (1-55713-027-2, $10.95)
My Poetry [in preparation]

MARY BUTTS [England]
Scenes from the Life of Cleopatra 72 (1-55713-140-6, $13.95)

OLIVIER CADIOT [France]
Art Poétique [in preparation]

PAUL CELAN [b. Bukovina/France]
Breathturn 74 (1-55713-218-6, $12.95)

LOUIS-FERDINAND CÉLINE [France]
Dances without Music, without Dancers, without Anything
   [in preparation]

CLARK COOLIDGE [USA]
The Crystal Text 99 (1-55713-230-5, $11.95)
Own Face 39 (1-55713-120-1, $10.95)
The Rova Improvisations 34 (1-55713-149-X, $11.95)
Solution Passage: Poems 1978–1981 [in preparation]
This Time We Are One/City in Regard [in preparation]

ROSITA COPIOLI [Italy]
The Blazing Lights of the Sun 84 (1-55713-195-3, $11.95)

RENÉ CREVEL [France]
Are You Crazy? [in preparation]
Babylon 65 (1-55713-196-1, $12.95)
Difficult Death [in preparation]

MILO DE ANGELIS [Italy]
Finite Intuition: Selected Poetry and Prose 65 (1-55713-068-X, $11.95)

HENRI DELUY [France]
Carnal Love 121 (1-55713-272-0, $11.95)

RAY DIPALMA [USA]
The Advance on Messmer [in preparation]
Numbers and Tempers: Selected Early Poems 24
   (1-55713-099-X, $11.95)

HEIMITO VON DODERER [Austria]
The Demons 13 (1-55713-030-2, $29.95)
Every Man a Murderer 66 (1-55713-183-X, $14.95)
The Merovingians [in preparation]

FANNY HOWE [USA]
  The Deep North 15 (1-55713-105-8, $9.95)
  Radical Love: A Trilogy [in preparation]
  Saving History 27 (1-55713-100-7, $12.95)

SUSAN HOWE [USA]
  The Europe of Trusts 7 (1-55713-009-4, $10.95)

LAURA (RIDING) JACKSON [USA]
  Lives of Wives 71 (1-55713-182-1, $12.95)

HENRY JAMES [USA]
  The Awkward Age [in preparation]
  What Maisie Knew [in preparation]

LEN JENKIN [USA]
  Dark Ride and Other Plays 22 (1-55713-073-6, $13.95)
  Careless Love 54 (1-55713-168-6, $9.95)
  Pilgrims of the Night: Five Plays [in preparation]

WILHELM JENSEN [Germany]
  Gradiva 38 (1-55713-139-2, $13.95)

JEFFREY M. JONES [USA]
  The Crazy Plays and Others [in preparation]
  J. P. Morgan Saves the Nation 157 (1-55713-256-9, $9.95)
  Love Trouble 78 (1-55713-198-8, $9.95)
  Night Coil [in preparation]

STEVE KATZ [USA]
  Florry of Washington Heights [in preparation]
  43 Fictions 18 (1-55713-069-8, $12.95)
  Swanny's Ways [in preparation]
  Wier & Pouce [in preparation]

ALEXEI KRUCHENYKH [Russia]
  Suicide Circus: Selected Poems [in preparation]

THOMAS LA FARGE [USA]
  Terror of Earth 136 (1-55713-261-5, $11.95)

VALERY LARBAUD [France]
  Childish Things 19 (1-55713-119-8, $13.95)

OSMAN LINS [Brazil]
  Nine, Novena 104 (1-55713-229-1, $12.95)

NATHANIEL MACKEY [USA]
  Bedouin Hornbook [in preparation]

JACKSON MAC LOW [USA]
  Barnesbook [in preparation]
  From Pearl Harbor Day to FDR's Birthday 126
    (0-940650-19-3, $10.95)
  Pieces O' Six 17 (1-55713-060-4, $11.95)
  Two Plays [in preparation]

CLARENCE MAJOR [USA]
  Painted Turtle: Woman with Guitar (1-55713-085-X, $11.95)

F. T. MARINETTI [Italy]
  Let's Murder the Moonshine: Selected Writings 12
    (1-55713-101-5, $13.95)
  The Untameables 28 (1-55713-044-7, $10.95)

HARRY MATHEWS [USA]
  Selected Declarations of Dependence (1-55713-234-8, $10.95)

FRIEDRIKE MAYRÖCKER [Austria]
  with each clouded peak [in preparation]

DOUGLAS MESSERLI [USA]
  After [in preparation]
  Ed. *50: A Celebration of Sun & Moon Classics* 50
    (1-55713-132-5, $13.95)
  Ed. *From the Other Side of the Century: A New American
    Poetry 1960–1990* 47 (1-55713-131-7, $29.95)
  Ed. [with Mac Wellman] *From the Other Side of the
    Century II: A New American Drama 1960–1995* [in preparation]
  River to Rivet: A Poetic Trilogy [in preparation]

DAVID MILLER [England]
  The River of Marah [in preparation]

CHRISTOPHER MORLEY [USA]
  Thunder on the Left 68 (1-55713-190-2, $12.95)

GÉRARD DE NERVAL [France]
  Aurelia [in preparation]

VALÈRE NOVARINA [France]
  The Theater of the Ears 85 (1-55713-251-8, $13.95)

CHARLES NORTH [USA]
  New and Selected Poems [in preparation]

TOBY OLSON [USA]
Dorit in Lesbos [in preparation]
Utah [in preparation]

MAGGIE O'SULLIVAN [England]
Palace of Reptiles [in preparation]

SERGEI PARADJANOV [Armenia]
Seven Visions [in preparation]

ANTONIO PORTA [Italy]
Metropolis [in preparation]

ANTHONY POWELL [England]
Afternoon Men [in preparation]
Agents and Patients [in preparation]
From a View to a Death [in preparation]
O, How the Wheel Becomes It! 76 (1-55713-221-6, $10.95)
Venusburg [in preparation]
What's Become of Waring [in preparation]

SEXTUS PROPERTIUS [Ancient Rome]
Charm 89 (1-55713-224-0, $11.95)

RAYMOND QUENEAU [France]
Children of Clay [in preparation]

CARL RAKOSI [USA]
Poems 1923–1941 64 (1-55713-185-6, $12.95)

TOM RAWORTH [England]
Eternal Sections 23 (1-55713-129-5, $9.95)

NORBERTO LUIS ROMERO [Spain]
The Arrival of Autumn in Constantinople [in preparation]

AMELIA ROSSELLI [Italy]
War Variations [in preparation]

JEROME ROTHENBERG [USA]
Gematria 45 (1-55713-097-3, $11.95)

SEVERO SARDUY [Cuba]
From Cuba with a Song 52 (1-55713-158-9, $10.95)

ALBERTO SAVINIO [Italy]
Selected Stories [in preparation]

LESLIE SCALAPINO [USA]
Defoe 46 (1-55713-163-5, $14.95)

PAUL VAN OSTAIJEN [Belgium/Flanders]
The First Book of Schmoll [in preparation]

CARL VAN VECHTEN [USA]
Parties 31 (1-55713-029-9, $13.95)
Peter Whiffle [in preparation]

TARJEI VESAAS [Norway]
The Great Cycle [in preparation]
The Ice Palace 16 (1-55713-094-9, $11.95)

KEITH WALDROP [USA]
The House Seen from Nowhere [in preparation]
Light While There Is Light: An American History 33
(1-55713-136-8, $13.95)

WENDY WALKER [USA]
The Sea-Rabbit or, The Artist of Life 57 (1-55713-001-9, $12.95)
The Secret Service 20 (1-55713-084-1, $13.95)
Stories Out of Omarie 58 (1-55713-172-4, $12.95)

BARRETT WATTEN [USA]
Frame (1971–1991) [in preparation]

MAC WELLMAN [USA]
The Land Beyond the Forest: Dracula AND *Swoop* 112
(1-55713-228-3, $12.95)
The Land of Fog and Whistles: Selected Plays [in preparation]
Two Plays: A Murder of Crows AND *The Hyacinth Macaw* 62
(1-55713-197-X, $11.95)

JOHN WIENERS [USA]
707 Scott Street 106 (1-55713-252-6, $12.95)

ÉMILE ZOLA [France]
The Belly of Paris 70 (1-55713-066-3, $14.95)